REFLECTED MUSIC
AND OTHER ESSAYS

REFLECTED MUSIC
AND OTHER ESSAYS

BY
BASIL MAINE

WITH A PREFACE BY
SIR HENRY WOOD

METHUEN & CO. LTD.
36 ESSEX STREET, W.C
LONDON

First Published in 1930

PRINTED IN GREAT BRITAIN

TO
EDNA AND IRENE

PREFACE

THIS book is welcome because it is at once serious and unprejudiced ; the author does not seek to amuse at the expense of reason and truth, and he is not a highbrow who has made up his mind that actual conditions are unworthy of his consideration.

The way in which he approaches the subject of wireless and gramophone music is characteristic. He has faced the fact that musicians must nowadays either take part in mechanical music or fall out of rank. He knows also that the public all the world over is listening to mechanical music and has made up its mind to hear more of it. Without prejudice, with an open mind and a broad outlook, Mr. Maine has accepted these conditions. Music, he realizes, must increasingly be made for the purpose of its conveyance to an enormous public unseen by the musician. Increasingly the artist will not be in direct touch with his audience, but will communicate with them through a mechanical medium.

It is music thus conveyed through a mechanism which Mr. Maine has made his special subject. This is all to the good. Thousands to-day are hearing music, perhaps not always of the best class or perfectly performed, who have never attended a concert or an opera, and who have not even a nodding acquaintance with either first-rate or second-rate composers. It is important that they should, as they listen, be stimulated to think as well as to feel. During my recent visits to Hollywood I was much struck by the fact that a small orchestra plays constantly while films are being made, and I was told that it is intended to induce the emotional atmosphere which may be absent when actors and actresses perform in silence. Music produces reactions which are now being experienced by countless multitudes of people for the first time. There is a danger that these reactions may not be intelligent enough, that we may listen to music too lazily now that we can hear it so easily. Therefore I welcome this book, which contains thoughts on music and especially on mechanical music. I hope that it may stimulate other listeners to follow its author's example and to make a certain intellectual effort after they have turned on the wireless or the gramophone.

HENRY J. WOOD

APPLE TREE FARMHOUSE
CHORLEY WOOD, HERTS
1929

CONTENTS

MY thanks are due to the Editors of the *Daily Telegraph*, the *Morning Post*, the *Sackbut* and the *Chesterian*, for permission to reprint some of the material of this book.

B. M.

REFLECTED MUSIC

THE power of the written word has never been so great as at this present time. Critics may be forgiven if, ever and anon, they pause to plume themselves awhile, when they realize that with every new discovery their sphere of influence is widened. The co-operation of criticism has been besought by each of a succession of scientific processes. Performance is becoming less and less immediate, and the attention of audiences is becoming more and more abstracted. Music, for instance, has been invaded by the gramophone, by the mechanical piano, and by broadcasting, and with each invasion criticism has been given fresh opportunity and impetus. It is not for critics to inquire why their opinions are so eagerly invited. What if the motive be entirely a commercial one ? We have no right to quarrel with a business man because he is business-like. And, quite apart from the commercial value of his work, the critic now finds that it is his duty to make himself intensely aware of what is happening around and above him. For example, the wonderful advance which has been made in gramophone reproduction during the last few years demanded the close and continual attention of experts, and the supply has not been far behind. Already there exists a healthy, full-grown journal which is devoted entirely to detailed and scientific criticism of recording processes, gramophone models and needle-points. And now it seems that broadcast music (and drama too) will be drawing official criticism into further toil and activity. This is as it should be. Broadcasting is the biggest revolution of this century. We have not yet begun to gauge or even to be aware of its far-reaching implications. Certainly the whole face of music will be changed under its influence. In another generation or two the majority of people will have quite a different idea of tone-colour from that which exists to-day. You may say that our ears will be made less subtle and sensitive, or that they will be unstopped. The fact remains that a change in our auditory sensations is inevitable. No critic can afford to be monastic in the face of this. He is but a fool who would shake the dust from off his feet, saying : ' If this is music, let me arise and go from hence and live in the Southern Isles, where I may hear no sound but the songs I make for myself.' We must live in our own time. Music is no longer a freely-springing well, but a self-conscious contrivance. It must needs take its colour from the civilization which surrounds it, and those who refuse to advance because the way is dark and narrow and uncertain are confessing their own weakness. They can have no part in the great inheritance.

Broadcast music, then, has every right to encounter serious criticism. When, however, we begin to formulate the principles governing this criticism, we find the usual difficulties. Try as we may to reduce critical procedure to an exact science, sooner or later we are driven to the conclusion that the most important quality in appraisement is personality, and this quality is the very antithesis of scientific methods. We may clear the ground, point out common fallacies, and even indicate a few immutable verdicts, but as soon as we begin to attempt application and construction we find that criticism is largely a matter of predilection and temperamental bias, and occasionally of unashamed caprice.

The chief difficulties in criticizing broadcast music are concerned with the mechanical means of transmission. Some time ago I complained that the advent of the gramophone had undammed a torrent of ignorant and incompetent music criticism. I contended that the functions of gramophone criticism should be divided between the man who knew how to get the best results and the man who knew how to criticize those results ; the one an engineer, the other a qualified musical critic. The mischief begins when the engineer leaves aside his expert knowledge of sound-boxes, needles, tone-arms, exponential horns, and the like, and tries his wings over the domain of purely musical values.

There is the same danger in the matter of

broadcast music—the danger that those who are thoroughly versed in the science of transmission will be tempted to assume a technical knowledge of that which is transmitted. After all, there is no reason why we should expect these individuals to know the subtleties of tonal intensity which go to make a perfect ensemble in string quartet playing. It is for the austere musical critic to say wherein there is success or blemish, and guided by his pronouncement, maybe the engineer will be able to observe and make perfect.

If the musical critic is to be of any value in this complex alliance, it goes without saying that his receiving-set must be the very best available, whether it is in his home or, as it has been suggested, in a receiving-room somewhere in the concert-hall district. Tentative criticism is worse than useless. When we read that in a broadcast performance of the ' Tannhäuser ' Overture the strings were obliterated by the brass-tone, we naturally assume that either the string-players and brass-players were out of proportion numerically or that they were wrongly placed. But when we read later on, ' At least, so I found it on my set, which I admit is not the latest model ', we are justified in complaining that the critic has wasted both his time and ours.

Taking it for granted, then, that the critic must suffer no impediment if his judgement is to hold value, how will he approach his work ? By what standard must he measure performance—according to reality or according to the conditions of the medium ? Most emphatically his standard must have relation to the special environment of the sounds he hears. For there can be little doubt that broadcast music will ultimately take its place as a definite entity, existing in its own rights. It will not be long before we speak of ' wireless music ' as we speak of ' violin music '— that is, as something which has a peculiar quality of its own, a quality which is conditioned by the instrument which it designedly employs. The only difference is that wireless music will employ two instruments, two media for its conveyance, just as on occasion the sun's light is reflected by the moon and then refracted by a shining cloud. Why should there not be as much beauty in reflected music as in reflected light ?

There is one aspect of broadcast music the importance of which we are in danger of minimizing. Since the beginning of 1927 we have been brought face to face with a new phenomenon in this country, namely, State music. It is not altogether true to say that the British Broadcasting Corporation is to be exploited by State Socialism. The Government has continually and carefully explained that it has done no more than establish an ' equitable trust ', and by this we understand that the public will receive its full share of the benefits that may accrue. Yet it is significant that the British Government, which formerly had resolutely refused to follow the examples of other European Governments in subsidizing music and drama, has now willingly undertaken the daily entertainment of the nation at large. So far as music is concerned, however, very little has been done to guarantee the wise and proper construction of programmes. After all, an advisory committee has no power to enforce its advice, and there is still no musician of authority in direct control.

This is alarming, in face of the probability that the B.B.C. will develop into a monopoly more extensive than any we have yet encountered in this country. The arrival of television is more than an awe-inspiring prophecy. It is more than likely that future generations will employ its opportunities and effects with no more wonder in their eyes than we have when we turn on the bath water or the Unfinished Symphony. And it is not fantastic to suppose that for those children as yet unborn, concert-going will be rendered unnecessary, if not undesirable. For them there will be no public music but that which is pre-scribed by the State, and since we are now content to submit our programmes to a body of people who are of all men avowedly the least musical, there is no reason to believe that they will have reached salvation in the interim. Rather will they be intoxicated with the power which has been vested in them so easily and uncritically. Clearly, then, we are entitled to demand the least of our rights. The sphere of politics is less sharply outlined than heretofore. Various interests have made themselves articulate in the body politic, and among them the interests of musicians have assumed real importance. But they have not yet gained unity and faith enough to make themselves clearly heard in the courts of representative government.

This is easily understood when we remember that in the development of parliamentary government, experience is the most important factor. Government in this country rested upon no security save personal tyranny until the knights of the shires came to Westminster to voice their needs and desires. Our representatives have never been brought face to face with the economic and other problems of the musical world, and we are taking far too optimistic a view of human nature if we expect them to attempt a solution on their own initiative. The only remedy lies in the willing co-operation of the Government and the people who care for these things. Until that co-operation is established, no good thing can come of State-ordained music.

THE WRITTEN WORD

AT the beginning of the previous essay I made reference to the growing power of the written word. Let me recur to that theme, for it is obviously of great importance.

Time was when there was real significance in the ancient proverb, ' Of thy unspoken word thou art master ; thy spoken word is master of thee.' But the significance has paled before the flamboyance of the present age. And as with the spoken word, so also with the written word. There was never a time when criticism was more widely practised than it is now. For every single event in the literary, theatre, art, or music world, a rough average of from twenty to forty men and women are employed to shape their views into some form of criticism. The first night of a new play and the first performance of a musical work are followed by the wild and rapid firing of the morning Press, by the slightly weightier considerations of the weekly journals, and then, perchance, by the mature wisdom of the monthlies and quarterlies. In addition there is always the likelihood that a ' question ' will arise and burn in the correspondence columns for some weeks. Even a Noel Coward play is used for profound speculation by the critics of those

weekly papers that are the special diet of the
upper middle level of intelligence. I was amused
to see, for instance, that Mr. Desmond McCarthy
gave three columns of precious space in the *New
Statesman* to a criticism of Coward's *The Queen
was in the Parlour*. Again, in the *Sunday Times*,
Mr. Ernest Newman devoted two successive
weeks to Mr. Paul Whiteman's book on ' Jazz.'
There is no real reason why journalistic space
should not be used in this way. A Bach fugue
and a Beethoven sonata teach us that it is not so
much the subject as the development which
ultimately counts, and Mr. Newman could write
about barbed wire and still be interesting. But
there is a grave danger that we shall lose our
sense of values in the midst of this riot of criticism.
As a result of the two instances I have given I am
sure that scores of people have received the
impression that *The Queen was in the Parlour* is as
important a contribution to contemporary English
drama as, say, Laurence Binyon's *The Young
King*, or John Masefield's *Melloney Holtspur*, and
hundreds of people (including ' the Jazz King '
himself) have an exaggerated idea of the importance of Mr. Paul Whiteman.

There are many reasons why the practice of
criticism has become so general, fluent, and light-
hearted. Composers, dramatists, performers,
authors, and artists—all have been compelled to
reflect the colour of a strictly utilitarian age, and
critics have followed in their train. There is no

help for it.   In theory, of course, the critic should
be standing over and above the mechanically
mercenary pursuits of the creative world—should
care for none of these things.   But, in reality,
this assumption is falsified at every turn, and the
quality of austerity, which should be the peculiar
mark of criticism, is rarely to be encountered.
Another symptom which is typical of these times
is the sanctification of performance.   It is more
blessed to perform than to conceive.   Here
again the critic has shared the weakness of his
fellows.

It is true that he cannot share in the immediate
reward of performance that comes to the
recitalist and the actor in the form of applause ;
but the expert critic will always be careful to
light upon a controversial subject so that he can
be certain of exciting some fiery antagonist to
unsheathe his pen with a martial flourish and
write a challenging letter to the editor.   These
letters are as vinegar and spice to the critic's
palate.   They whet his appetite for the devouring
of page after page of manuscript.   They also
enable him to visualize his scattered audience
and give him a sense of contact.   In short, they
encourage him to play the rôle of performer and
often at the expense of his purely critical faculty.
For the act of performance and the act of criticism
have little in common.   The performer must score
points and ' get effects ', as the saying goes ;
he must lead the unwary audience into believing

that for the moment he is the only man who counts in his particular line. Whether he be tragedian or comedian, singer or juggler, violinist or acrobat, he must constantly be feeling the pulse of his audience ; he must observe their mood, and if there be any signs of flagging or restlessness he must at any cost regain undivided attention, the comedian with ' some excellent jest fire-new from the mint ', the singer with some excellent tone of unusual vibration.   On the other hand the critic, that is to say the ideal critic, will be unmindful of everything save the subject of his criticism.   He is the searcher after truth, and for the moment he cares not who else believes so long as he can persuade himself.   The audience with him is a secondary consideration ; indeed, even if it were abolished entirely, the essential quality of his preoccupation would remain.

As I have hinted above, the functions of performance and criticism are rapidly being merged ; and the time seems not distant when they will be perfectly congruent.   It is true that the first (London) performances of works like Stravinsky's *Les Noces* or Honegger's *King David* are anticipated because of the composers' reputations and the intrigue which is attendant upon them ; but it is hardly an exaggeration to say that the eagerness is conditioned just as much by speculation as to what judgement the critics will deliver.   The best part of the fun of producing a new Stravinsky work is to read Mr. Ernest

Newman on the subject on the following Sunday.
In the opinion of a great number of people, his
performance is at least equal in importance to
the actual performance of the work.   If you have
attended any of the big provincial festivals (at
Leeds or at Norwich, or the Three Choirs) you will
know how impossible it is to hold converse with
your friends before eleven o'clock in the morning.
They take up an unassailable position behind the
columns of the morning Press and no amount of
persuasion will tempt them to come forth into
the open.   There is significance in all this.   It
means that the close association of musical
activity with journalism has brought about a
radical change in the nature of criticism.   It is
useless to cry out against that which is inevitable.
Journalism has created a demand for performing
critics, and the musical profession has been only
too ready to meet the demand.   Nor need we
assume that the written word will lose its unique
power among men, merely because the profession
of musical criticism (and of all criticism) is open
to anybody who has a talent for entertainment ;
for the fact that there is a large public willing and
anxious to read about music—so large that even
the low-brow and the no-brow journals admit the
necessity of employing experts to write on musical
events—argues a much higher standard of general
intelligence on the part of the public ; and from
this we may deduce that the sham critic who
seeks to deceive his readers with a few rapid

passes and an incessant flow of patter will be easily discovered and disowned.

Nevertheless, the danger of critics mistaking their function is a very real one, and they need constantly to be on the alert lest they deceive themselves, and with themselves the very elect. For, when all is said, the power of criticism is the power to enlighten, and not merely the power to amuse. Beyond this there is no sure way of defining the nature of criticism. But it is possible to cite passages in which true criticism can be felt at work. Not long ago I encountered an article in which the art of appraisement was admirably revealed. The subject was ' Two Paintings of the Baptism by Paul Veronese ', and within a brief space the writer (Detler Baron von Hadeln) gave a clear and simple exposition of the earlier and later styles of Veronese, an exposition which brought to me—a layman where pictures are concerned—a new understanding and a sense of values. Because this article contained no corruption of words, no searching after effect, no conscious desire to entertain, but instead a swiftly delivered stroke of judgement, I accepted it as a good and faithful example of what all criticism should be—a just valuation of things perceived.

THE VOCALIZED WORD

(This essay is intended to be read aloud)

HUMAN relationship depends upon a variety of subtle qualities—upon poise, gait, carriage, facial expression, manner of thought, manner of speech, and all the subdivisions which these things imply.

But it would be difficult to establish that any one of these attributes has more power to draw or repel, to heal or annoy, than the voice, whether it employs the comparatively level tones of ordinary speech, the fervour of oratory, or the rhapsody of song.

The loveliness of eyes is a constant lure to the lonely of heart ; but they inspire fear rather than love, for they are used, especially by women, to deceive rather than to express.

The mouth, too, is more frequently a mechanical medium for superficial charm or a mask for motive than a revelation of truth. Even a hand-grasp can be shamefully and painfully exaggerated.

But the voice can shield no generous or sinister design ; it is in such close contact with the fundamental emotions that it cannot trifle with realities. It is the very sum and the audible evidence of personality. It is possible to fall in love with a voice, quite apart from all its fleshly appurtenances. It is just as possible to hold an unswerving hatred of the voice of a person otherwise held in affection.

The swift and relentless developments of civilization, that are the chief characteristics of this present era, are tending to bring the human voice into greater prominence than ever before. There are countless pairs of people who have never met and yet are perfectly well known to each other over the telephone.

Think of the enormous expansion of the sphere of influence over which a singer holds sway through the revolutions of a gramophone record. Even more immediate is the contact established between an individual and a diverse and widespread audience through broadcasting.

If it were absolutely necessary the Prime Minister could, at a time of crisis, address the whole of the electorate while taking his bath. Obviously this aerial method of intercourse is tending to throw a heavy responsibility upon the voice, and it is becoming increasingly urgent for those people who have entertainment to offer, or criticism to publish, or commands to give, to make fine the art of vocalization.

At the present time, however, the art of voice production (I am referring both to singing and speaking) is at a sad discount in this country. I expect this remark to provoke many protests.

The reader will at once seek about in his mind

for refutations, and will quote this or that singer, actor, politician, or even those invisible and endeared announcers who call upon us nightly from 2LO. But who shall deny that these are the very exceptions that prove my charge ? We, who dutifully but reluctantly attend the unbroken succession of recitals given in London, know full well that the average singer of to-day is—save the mark !—a thing of naught.

As for speaking, the average Englishman is almost ashamed to enunciate clearly, lest he should be accounted a pedant, or, what is worse, a snob. The English stage is in a most lamentable state of disrepair in this connexion.

I well remember something that Mary Anderson said to me after a production of a Masefield play. This was her remark : ' Thank goodness, we could hear the words. You know, there is hardly any fine speaking on the English stage at the present time. Actors and actresses are so busy being natural that they overlook the most natural thing in the world—clear speech.'

I am not the one to echo and elaborate an outcry which has already been made sufficiently forcible by a stronger voice than mine—by Mr. St. John Ervine, in fact. I merely wish to record my distress, and in the midst of it to muse upon a few occasions when my despair has been lightened a little. There are three blessings that I could count. The first is the blessing of John McCormack's singing. Here is a man who, with the upward gesture of his voice, can transport a multitude of people. You object that he uses his talent for trading in the tinsel of balladry. What is that to me? I am not concerned with the commercial conditions which react upon a singer's life.

I only know that I have heard McCormack sing 'Giote al canto mio', from Peri's *Euridice*, and for a brief moment have thought myself in possession of a great, unutterable secret. Even when he stoops he adorns. He sings 'When Twilight Comes I'm Thinking of You', and clothes its wretchedness with the graceful folds of an Italian aria.

Then there is Henry Ainley. I confess myself old-fashioned enough to take an uncritical delight in his rich and finely-modulated tones, in spite of the fact that his voice and manner are 'impersonated' at every smoking-concert.

Thirdly, let me sing of Florence Mills—whose voice beguiled, as it were any enraptured bird, whatsoever its plumage or lineage; beguiled, and saddened too, for the tones of it were all 'with pathos delicately edged'. Her *coloratura* was as wide in range, as flexible in movement, as clean and sure in flight and descent as that of any ascetic *prima donna*. But she was not, as each of them is, a performing nightingale.

She never performed—she merely reacted to the delight of making a joyful sound. I recall with what alarm I was seized, when she told me that she was intending to take singing lessons. ' Don't,' I begged of her ; ' you will never smile again.' Whereat she frowned a little and looked wistful, and said she would consider my advice.

OPERA RECONSIDERED

I. OPERA AS A FORM OF ART

IS opera, as a form of art, absurd ? Many
there are who think so, and it is necessary
from time to time to make inquiry, lest they
find the opposite case defenceless, and lest we
find it untenable.

The word ' absurd ' is violent in the extreme.
It implies a ruthless condemnation ; it also
implies a persistence on the part of the thing
condemned—a persistence which is most disturbing to those who indulge in preconceptions
about life and its affairs. The persistence of
the form of art which is known as opera is a
constant inconvenience to those who have applied
the better part of their mental activity to
the meticulous construction of theories ; for
by no stretch of imagination or of toleration
can this hybrid thing be accounted for or fully
explained.

Yet at the moment the thing is certainly not
dead, although there are signs, as I have shown
elsewhere, that contemporary composers are becoming discontented with opera as a medium for
expression. It continues to exist, spite of all the
slings and arrows of the outrageous music-hall

comedian, spite of the taunts of the foolish and
the rebukes of the wise. For three hundred years
and more composers have turned instinctively to
opera, knowing full well that they were courting
disaster. Their continuous activity is a difficult
and indivisible factor in the terms of the proposi-
tion. It cannot be ignored if the solution is to be
final, since it implies that there is some unsub-
stantial thing which music lacks and which drama
lacks, but which, peradventure, can be supplied
by their willing co-operation. And since opera
can neither be ignored nor destroyed, obviously
the only thing left for those who require immediate
satisfaction is to take extreme measures. The
word ' absurd ' expresses the extremity both of
their failure and of their indignation.

There is nothing more simple than to base a
condemnation upon the magnifying of details—
upon deliberate distortion. I shall not be so
bold as to deny the utter absurdity of certain
operatic situations. Indeed, I accept them
willingly as the necessary material for the
construction of my own case. An entity does
not necessarily repeat the qualities of its com-
ponent parts. Because an incident in an opera is
absurd it does not follow that the whole work is
absurd ; nor are we justified in declaring the
whole course of operatic development to be an
utterly foolish expedition because of the ignominious failure of certain individual works. Just
as we are in error to deny the success of *The Rose*

Cavalier as a work because some of the dialogue in the first act misses fire, so are we mistaken in judging the history of opera to be a tale of futile endeavour merely because it includes such sad misconceptions as *Pianella* and *The Bohemian Girl*.

There is no charge easier to bring and support against human activity than that of absurdity. For what, after all, is the cause of the innumerable little absurdities to which we are prone ? The cause, almost invariably, is a sudden twist of normal perspective. When we look at human beings as they are reflected by a convex mirror, idiosyncrasies become abnormalities, and we are shocked by the sudden realization of what might have been. We are no longer aware of the context, so to speak, but only of the single feature made absurd by being deprived of its proper relationship to the scheme of things. In other words, absurdity, like dirt, is a condition of things. Dirt is matter out of place ; absurdity, in like manner, is material out of place. Now, this condition of things—the condition that creates absurdity—is more often than not due to the point from which they are viewed. A perfectly ordinary situation can be made to seem incoherent nonsense by being put ever so slightly out of focus. A well-dressed man claims the right to walk the length of Bond Street in a leisurely way. The exercise of this prerogative is an event ordinary enough in its way. But let there be the smallest

disturbance in the ensemble—the omission of part
of the man's clothing (the collar, let us say), and
the event is at once whisked off to another plane
—' to a plane ', as Mr. Yeats might have written
in a loose moment :

> To a plane where even the proud are fun
> And even the Correct are hopelessly out.

It is an easy thing to create such a situation even
when it does not exist, and those who bring the
charge of absurdity against opera make light of
their task and present it from such an oblique
angle that it is difficult to regain a normal vision.
They are constantly examining the case through
the wrong end of the opera glasses.

It is but natural that opera, which is a com-
pounding of two arts, should constantly lie open
to the charge of absurdity.   The perfect opera is
outside the range of man's imagination.   At any
given moment it is almost certain that one or
other of the elements will be in ascendancy, unless
both are in abeyance.   And on the rare occasions
when the fusion of the dramatic action and the
musical progression is satisfactorily accomplished
—as for example in the Othello-Iago dialogue in
the second act of Verdi's opera—then it is more
than likely that the delicate balance will be upset
by some indelicate emphasis on the part of the
actors.   (And here, in parenthesis, I should like to
emphasize that the absurdity of operatic acting

is a condition which has been superimposed upon opera, and is in no wise essential to its nature and continued existence.   But of this, more anon). And yet, in spite of these countless and overwhelming criticisms against opera as a feasible form of art, it is necessary for us to give some satisfactory reason for its continued appeal.   It is also necessary for us to account in some way for its first beginning.

At some time or other, somebody or other, for some reason or other, called in music as an aid to the illusion of the theatre.   It is not dangerous to assume that the reason for this summons was that a certain kind of dramatic situation could not be fully realized without music.   Here we have the first and chief function of music in the theatre, namely, to intensify and transcend dramatic situation and development.   From this two other functions follow in natural sequence.   The first is that of characterization, which is arrived at through an assiduous employment of the laws of association ;   the second is to give the drama its proper setting, ' to create an atmosphere ', as we are fond of saying.   In the carrying out of this duty, music must be willing to forfeit its self-sufficiency, but not necessarily so far as to be utterly without meaning apart from the theatre, as we see very clearly from the popularity of the Wagner excerpts in the concert hall.   With these three definite and necessary duties to perform it cannot be said that music is an impostor in the theatre. Nor could composers be accused of encroaching upon preserves when they extended their sphere of influence from mere incidental music to coincidental music, from the music of running comment to the music of interpretation. They were following an instinct as true and compelling as the instinct of life itself, for the tendency of all the finest drama is towards poetic utterance, and the tendency of all the finest poetry is towards the state of music. What, then, could be more natural and generous than that composers should place themselves at the disposal of the theatre whenever an imperfection was felt or an impediment encountered ?

That the imperfection is sometimes mended and that the impediment is sometimes removed is witnessed by those experiences which we cannot define more exactly than as the ' great moments ' of opera. When the composer is also a man of the theatre, as Mozart, Verdi, and Puccini were (I am deliberately omitting Wagner here in order to keep the issue clear), the alliance of music and drama is justified by master-stroke after master-stroke. The effect may be merely exclamatory, or it may be episodic, but it is always of that kind which could not have been brought about by the single operation of either music or drama. The nature of these culminating effects eludes analysis, but if we exclude Puccini for a moment we may say that, so far from being physical, it is actually metaphysical and, on occasions, even mystical.

To those who are willing to follow or to be led, these culminations bring a moment of intense awareness, of sudden great ecstasy. The behaviour of individuals at such moments varies with the degree of their understanding. For some there is no way but to cry aloud with indecent joy ; others prefer to bear their convulsion in silence, unless they take steps to rebuke those who have disturbed the enjoyment of their secretly suppressed rebellion. But to both these groups opera signifies a transcending of ordinary events and relationships ; they are willing to overlook the incongruous elements, the little absurdities, which have been subtly compounded for their pleasure, since in the light of experience they are assured that those elements will finally be transfigured and made gloriously eloquent.

Therefore let those whose sensibilities are more fastidious, and whose receptivity is less ample, refrain from casting the pebbles of ridicule, lest they themselves should be hit by one, rebounding.

2. ACTING IN OPERA

It is easy to fell a habit of mind, but almost impossible to uproot it. So often the roots are the very fibres of our being ; in such cases the habit may be said to be essential to the life. But there are other habits, no less difficult to disentangle from everyday existence, which are excrescences, false creations, unreal realities. These are usually the complex result of individual heredity, environment, and temperamental bias. When we find such habits transferred from the individual to the community, it is reasonable to expect that in the process of transference they will become weakened or diluted, or made less definite. But the opposite is true. A crowd instinct is a much more powerful force than an individual instinct, in spite of the diversity of elements—antagonistic elements, maybe—which have gone towards its composition.

So we find certain customs, traditions, and manners persisting changelessly through changing generations. On the face of it they are absurd, but they continue, not in spite, but because, of their absurdity. Human nature is only too eager to endow the incongruous with some supposed quality of mystery and sacredness. The results appear in such anomalies as capital punishment, golf, English Sundays, cocktail parties, and operatic acting. Any one of these subjects provides material for a protest to the extent of a full-dress essay, but, for my part, I find that none of them excites in me so much wrathful indignation as the last, and it is to that I would devote a little of your attention, since the mood is upon me.

Acting in opera ! The term is almost a contradiction in itself. We do not associate opera with acting, or, rather, we associate it with that grossly exaggerated form of gesture and expression, the skitting of which is the last resource of the music-hall comedian and the revue sketch. The stage conduct of an opera singer is not so much acting as ' finding something to do '. The trouble is that the average opera singer begins to busy himself about finding something to do just at the very moment when the composer is doing it for him, either in the orchestral score or in the direction of the vocal line. The sense of repose is the rarest of all the stage senses—and this is true not only of the opera house but of the whole theatre. The amazing thing is that the person who would profit most by reposing, even for a few consecutive seconds, is the very one who insists upon introducing all kinds of extraneous irrelevant activity, thereby increasing a task already sufficiently difficult in itself. That this activity *is* extraneous and irrelevant can be shown by a simple test which is applicable to any operatic situation : let the singers repeat the scene without the music and let them speak their lines, using the same gestures and movements which they saw fit to use while singing ! The result was cruelly made manifest in a recent revue, wherein the sextet from *Lucia* was submitted to the process.

There is, of course, an immediate objection to this kind of analysis. Opera is nothing if not the embodiment of all that is most intense. The very fact that music was called into the theatre at all, reveals that there was felt the need of lifting the emotional significance of the drama above the ordinary plane. The need may have been real or only apparent ; the point is that it was felt. You and I and other perceptive people do not feel that anything can be added to the music of Shakespeare's balcony scene in *Romeo and Juliet* ; but Jules Barbier, Michael Carré and Charles Gounod had the idea that, together, they could add half a cubit or so to the stature of that mighty conception. And the trouble is that a few people have always felt that way about the drama. Hence the evolution of that form which is called opera—a form so awkward that it refuses to fit in with our preconceived theories of art, however anxious we may be to accommodate its presence. On the other hand, its influence and power are sufficient to resist the fiercest attack or the deadliest thrust of satire.

Therefore, since opera continues to stand in its own right, and since its special claim is that it exists to intensify and make resplendent the stress of ordinary emotion, it follows that it has the right to evolve its own special technique or system of behaviour. The behaviour of a Shakespearean Othello in the scene beginning ' Thou hast set me on the rack ' cannot be taken as it stands and applied to the same scene of Verdi's opera. It is at once too subtle and too finely organized. The singing actor must think first

of his singing and afterwards of his acting. If
the acting can be co-ordinated with the singing,
it is well ; if not, then a series of signs must be
employed to assure the audience that he has not
been suddenly thwarted by paralysis. And so
the vast, intricate, unshakable edifice of operatic
traditions is gradually built up. Singers must
know not only the music of their rôles and of the
other rôles associated with them, but they must
learn a cyclic series of sacred signs and wonders
which are grouped together under the eloquent
word ' business '. At a certain point in the
Hagen-Gunther-Gutrune conference, for example,
Gunther must rise from his position back-left of
the stage, and walk across to the footlights-right ;
then, seeing that he can walk no farther, turn
indignantly on his heel, and move to back-right.
We should not object to this perambulation so
much if it did not always suggest that Gunther
regarded the stage as a chess-board and himself
as a knight for whom certain squares and pro-
gressions were forbidden.

We can cede the point that opera must needs
develop its own technique of acting, but the fact
remains that technique which draws attention to
itself defeats its own end.

But the most flagrantly absurd of all operatic
' business ' is that associated with the great
love-duets. By this the very object of opera is
frustrated ; for how can the most compelling of
all human emotions be intensified by the sight

of two people addressing themselves, not to each
other, but to the audience, and employing the
kind of frantic gesture which we associate with
extreme distress ?   How often does it happen
that the fervour of fine singing in the Sieglinde-
Siegmund scene of *Die Walküre* is impeded
by the tyranny of this ' business '—this urgent
necessity of being busy when there is nothing
whatever to do except sing of an ecstasy so
delicately static that the slightest movement
disturbs its spell ?   I hold my soul in patience
until the day when I shall encounter singers wise
enough and courageous enough to express this
scene and all the other passionate scenes of opera
with a minimum of bodily disturbance.   The only
excuse for permitting the musical expression of
a dramatic situation is that the situation can
be conveyed by no less drastic a means with so
great a force.   Otherwise the composer is poaching upon preserves.   So also with the composer's
employees.   If the singers cannot communicate
the full significance of the Fidelio-Florestan or the
Tristan-Isolde duets through the uplift of their
voices alone, then it is merely confessing and
revealing failure to fall back upon the traditional
presenting-of-arms.

This is not to argue that the only safe way in
opera is for the singer to appear as one who is tied
to the stake.   The negation of movement is the
other extremity, and one almost as ludicrous in
effect, as we see from the enforced inaction of

Parsifal.   His is not so much a sense of repose as a sense of nothing.   The average operatic situation demands from the characters an awareness of themselves and their environment which can be conveyed by no amount of guileless fooling. Nor can it be expressed by reactions which are out of the range of human reason and decorum. There is always the way of moderation, economy and restraint.   The first steps along that way can be indicated by the following injunctions : (1) Let all Wagnerian singers learn to walk the stage naturally and without calling attention to the fact that they are consciously obeying an instruction printed in the score.   (2) In cases where a concerted movement is definitely an intrusion and a distraction, let there be a simplification.   It is nothing short of miraculous that three singers can ever be found to sing the Rhinemaidens' music, rocked as they must be in their cradles of the deep.   The scene could be produced just as effectively by a simple system of lighting, without the help of those shirt-sleeved assistants who, from the upper boxes of Covent Garden, can be seen running about with the preoccupied air of small boys flying large kites. (3) Let all arm signalling be suppressed, and, when two are gathered together in order to commune, let them become transfigured before us by the spirit of their singing.   We should be entirely unaware of the bodily aspect of their transport.   The technique of love-making on the

3

stage is an exceedingly sensitive organization, requiring the entire attention of the participants. Since opera singers cannot give their whole attention to the outward and visible sign, it is necessary that they should concentrate upon the audible sign, and make no attempt to represent the other. Even the final embrace should be forbidden, since, without the carefully prepared illusion of the finest acting, it is never anything but a shock. (4) Let there be no self-assertion in the ranks of the chorus. Those precocious individuals who find they have a talent for ' acting ' should be relegated to the back of the stage, where their amateur efforts cannot be seen ; that is, if the producer finds that they can be repressed by no stern measure of discipline.

And, if there be anyone who holds that the traditions of operatic acting represent a crystallization of the experience of the ages, and ought not to be changed by one iota, then let him attend a performance of Donizetti's *L'Elisir d'Amore* as given by the Teatro delle Piccole Maschere. The delicate wit of those spirited and nimble-bodied puppets mercilessly exposes the tinsel of operatic garments and reveals that the qualification of the word ' Opera ' by the word ' Grand ' is but a vain and unnecessary boast.

ACCORDING TO THE PROPHETS

'WHAT Mr. Roger Fry calls Art, I call Confectionery.' It is hardly necessary to tell you who was responsible for that statement. However bold and tantalizing his words may be, Mr. Bernard Shaw is never guilty of saying anything that might have been said by another.

The great value of his observations lies not so much in their truth as in the fact that they cause truth in others. He has a way of pouncing upon a platitude, and seizing it with his teeth ; then he shakes it violently to prove to us that it is quite dead, if, indeed, it ever was alive. That word ' confectionery ' startles at first. It seems to be a deliberate taunt. But after a while it occurs to one that the word is only used to pursue and kill once more that dead old fox of a platitude ' Art is a mechanical process '.

Mr. Shaw makes quite certain of the kill this time ; the only objection is that he implies that Mr. Fry has been guilty of administering artificial respiration to a fallacy long deceased. In Mr. Fry's recently published essays on Art, I can find no statement which could be twisted into that

35

fallacy.   Here in a few words is the substance of his creed : ' I believe that in nearly every one, wherever a psychological appeal is possible, this is more immediately effective, more poignant than the plastic, but that with prolonged familiarity it tends to evaporate and leave plasticity as a more permanent, less rapidly exhausted, motive force.   So that when pictures survive for a long period their plastic appeal tends to count more and more in each succeeding generation.'

This assumption can be taken as a foundation for a theory of all the arts.   It has a special application to music.   Indeed, it is even more eloquently witnessed by musical than by pictorial compositions.   If it is true, for example, that the *Don Juan* of Strauss continues to stir us after a dozen hearings, it is certainly not because of the programmatic basis of the music, for that hardly bears a single repetition.   The appeal is made in some way or other through the musical design of the work.   The design of a given work may depend upon an intellectual or an emotional process—in *Don Juan* the appeal is chiefly to the emotions—but in either case we become aware of the quality which for the sake of definition we may call ' beauty in design '.   And it is precisely because the *Alpine Symphony* lacks that co-relation within itself, that significance of formal beauty, that it ceases to hold our attention as soon as we decide that the prospect of an uneventful mountain-climb is an insufficient spur to prick on our purely musical intent. In the same way the failure of a great amount of theatre music to become established in the concert-hall repertory is clearly accounted for ; and if you point to Wagner as an exception to this rule, he is so because his music promotes both the intellectual and the emotional processes, and never ceases to interest through the endless series of its mass, line, and colour relations.

Perhaps we shall never be permitted to penetrate the mystery of the relation which is called Beauty with the blunt point of a verbal definition. But we apprehend something of its nature when we realize its effect, which Mr. Fry describes in these words: ' Our reaction to works of art is a reaction to a relation and not to sensations or objects or persons or events,' and we travel even further when we admit that all aesthetic experience presupposes and is conditioned by this relation. (I am here accepting Professor Abercrombie's definition of aesthetic experience as experience which does not look outside itself for its value.) Furthermore, when aesthetic experience is submitted to the process of expression in a work of art, the relationship of the various parts within the experience will find a counterpart in the composition of the work.

It disturbs the poise and natural sequence of events to say that Rembrandt or Dante or Mozart ' confected ' their works, for this implies

artifice, anxious forethought, and a lack of
sensitiveness and receptivity, the very qualities
which we do not find in an artist. No great
work of art has been deliberately confected. It
is in the first place the result of the orderliness
of the artist's experience. That is what we call
' vision '. In the second place, it is the result
of the orderliness of the artist's thought and
purpose. That is ' inspiration '. Finally, it is
the result of the orderliness of the artist's work.
That is ' technique '. Inferior music, painting,
or literature owes its inferiority to the fact that
one or other of these causes is missing. If only
the first two are present we get inarticulate
works, such as those which Beethoven wrote
towards the end of his life ; if the last two are
present to the exclusion of the first, we get mere
' cleverness ', such as is found in much of our
contemporary music, and in this connexion we
may be justified in bringing the odious charge of
' confection '. It is obviously impossible to find
an example in which Vision and Technique are
present, and Inspiration absent, for without
purpose there can be no creation in art.

When Mr. Fry emphasizes the element of plastic
design in pictures, and gives out that it is ultimately of far greater value than psychological
and other incidental considerations, I do not
understand him, as Mr. Shaw seems to understand him, to be extolling technique as the greatest
gift in an artist. For the element of plasticity

is continually recurring throughout the various stages which lead up to the final act of creation. Without it, aesthetic experience is entirely insignificant, seeing that in that case it cannot be distinguished from any other experience.

So then, as I see it, Mr. Fry stands justified in stressing that which is most permanent, and therefore most valuable, in any work of art. And his theory is especially justified by musical experience, for it supplies a fairly satisfactory explanation of the eclipse of some composers and the survival of others. Bach's survival, for instance, is not due merely to a high degree of technical attainment. It is due to the fact that Bach's mind, whether in the act of receiving, conceiving or creating, never failed to exercise its own essential orderliness. He not only thought, but he ' experienced ' in terms of design and perfect relation. Chaos was a word without meaning to him. And another was Confectionery.

2.   H. G. WELLS

In this world of easy-going opinion we are occasionally reminded of the questions ' which every intelligent man should answer for himself '. Mr. H. G. Wells is never tired of discussing these cardinal issues. He is constantly disturbing the Sabbath calm of the *Sunday Express* public by reviving a number of awkward subjects, and treating them in such a way that we have no alternative but to conclude that all men are hypocrites. Lately he has been allowing the dazzling beam of his mind to play once more upon the subject of vivisection. There is one passage in his essay which can be profitably removed from its context and still retain significance in another application—a process which in itself can be likened to a vivisection experiment. Here is the passage :

'Vivisection is only occasionally and incidentally the infliction of pain, and anti-vivisection is not really a campaign against pain at all. The real campaign is against the thrusting of a scientific probe into mysteries and hidden things which it is felt should either be approached in a state of awe, tenderness, excitement or passion, or else avoided.'

Without taking sides about this statement—which, after all, is by no means axiomatic, in spite of the dogmatic form of the expression—it is possible to apply the principles which are implied to the creative impulse in contemporary music. Wherever we look we find the two uncompromising groups ; the one consisting of those who are for ever probing into mysteries, the other consisting of those who cry ' Let alone ; let us see what miracle will happen '.

The first group can bring strong arguments for its support. Those who have joined have the courage, not so much of their convictions as of their very beings. They are made that way. They can cite all the great pioneers of the past—Monteverdi, Bach, Beethoven, Wagner—men who were never content to stand in awe, but who were continually experimenting with that which was established, in order—not to disestablish—but to enlarge the establishment. For them the world of sound was not so boundless that it was hopeless to attempt the mapping of its lands and the charting of its seas ; or, if indeed it *did* seem boundless, there was no strong reason why it should not be made finite for the utilitarian purpose of composing music. The present position is that composers have reached the boundaries which have been prescribed by their forerunners, and are eager to press on to new territory in order to make settlement thereupon. If we fall back again upon the parallel of vivisection, we may say that they have taken the living body of Music, and, having given it an anaesthetic, have subjected it to all manner of dissecting experiments. The whole-tone scale was an experiment upon Tonality ; the quarter-tone system is an experiment upon ' Equal Temperament ' ; atonality is an experiment upon the whole face of Music as we have recognized it up till now. Those who take an active part in these experiments, whether it be anaesthetizing or actual surgery, claim that the pain involved is fully justified by the advance which is thereby made in the scientific region of music. The fact that the pain is not a direct infliction upon music itself but an indirect infliction upon those who hear it, does not materially lessen the value of the parallel, since the term ' Music ' must necessarily include the audience.

Those, on the other hand, who have set themselves against these fearless explorers can bring an equal amount of evidence to support their case. Some base their arguments entirely upon the ground that any music which causes a discomforting auditory sensation is at once excluded from the literal meaning of the term Music. Others—and these have the stronger position— give out that music which is purely the result of experiment is of no value whatever. These are the real anti-vivisectionists. They are old-fashioned enough to believe in Inspiration, and in the light of their belief they hold that the wide, feverish, complex activity which we are pleased to call Contemporary Music can be summed up by the single word Expiration. It is so much waste of breath, they would say, and would give as their reason that the composer of to-day is unwilling to wait for the silence through which music can be distilled into his spiritual ear. He must be eternally analysing, contriving, projecting ; he must also be continually explaining himself, lest there should be the slightest error in future experiments along the same line. And if they would make their argument more complete the anti-vivisectionists could make great play with the documentary evidence contained in the letter written by Alban Berg to his master Schönberg, explaining the nature of a composition which the pupil had written to honour his master's fiftieth birthday. When the blind must lead the blind, how exceeding great is the darkness!

This conflict between those who insist upon the emotional nature of music and those who insist upon its essentially intellectual nature has not arisen for the first time. But the contention has never been so acute as at the present time, and it is surprising to find how few are the members of the musical public who have definitely made up their minds on the point. It is all the more surprising when we realize the simplicity and clarity of the issue. Mr. Wells with his ' let's have no nonsense about it ' manner has expressed it admirably in these words : ' The world that the pro-vivisectionist is by his nature compelled to strip bare, the anti-vivisectionist clothes in rich swathings of feeling and self-protection.'

3. LAURENCE BINYON

Not long ago Mr. Laurence Binyon contributed to a musical paper an article which was in the nature of a confession. In the article, this sentence occurred : ' Expression in music is less conditioned by material (is it not ? I speak in ignorance) than in the other arts.' A writer in the *Manchester Guardian* was prompted by this observation to write as follows : ' The solemn truth is that composers of the present time are fretting in large numbers at the peculiar tyranny exercised over them by music's material, its " sounding air." Because music is a unique language, because so far it has lived mainly in a world beyond words, it has been driven to seek intelligibility by cultivating abstract form to a point that might easily breed art much too good for human nature's daily food.' Then he goes on to hold out a hope for the human-all-too-human composer—for him who desires to establish a definite relationship between his art and the common round of daily life. He uses such phrases as ' a means of escape from an air that is rather too divine, from an ether that is much too ample ', to reveal without shame his radical heart. The end of the argument is concerned with an attempt to show that speech and music are alike in this, that both are based upon an arbitrary connexion between ideas and their expression. But the reasoning is a little too good to be true ; it is not quite so easy as that. Or perhaps it would be more to the point to say that it ought not to be so easy ; for the sterility of so much contemporary music is undoubtedly due to the fact that composers have no courage to try their wings in that ' too ample ether ', and are content

to subject their art to a utilitarian and platitudin-
izing process. To say that there is a danger of
music becoming 'much too good' for daily
consumption is to utter two falsities in a single
breath. The statement implies that music is a
commodity which must be delivered, prepared,
and served at regular intervals for human sus-
tenance ; whereas, in point of fact, we know that
most of us are aurally too delicate to be able to
make a hearty meal at every sound of the
concert-agent's dinner-gong. It also implies that
the intrinsic value of music is to be judged by
a subjective rather than an objective process.
We have arrived at a sorry state of affairs
when a musical work is to be condemned
because 'we, you, or they' are not in a position to enumerate it among the real necessities
of life.

When the *Manchester Guardian* contributor
writes that composers have been driven to seek
intelligibility through abstract form, because
music happens to be an idiomatic language, he
is guilty of redundancy, and a certain amount of
perversion. We gain no enlightenment from the
statement that an archangel is an archangelic
being, and are rather confused when we are told
that an archangel has been driven to seek his
present state because of his archangelic qualities.
One would have thought it unnecessary to declare
what has been obvious almost from the beginnings
of music—from the very time when primitive

man beat his drum in fear or wailed to express
his exceeding joy—that music, being beyond all
verbal utterance, sought its own means of expression—was not driven to do so, but did so gladly
and of its own free will.   And when we finally
arrive at what is known as ' sonata form ', it is
clear that the composers who used that form did
not use it *faute de mieux*, but because it was a
natural growth from all that had gone before.
Therefore this alleged fretting of contemporary
composers under the yoke of abstraction is not
to be taken as a sign of health and vigour, but
of decadence.   For we do wrong to associate
decadence always with inertia ; feverish reaction
can lead men just as surely to a dying fall.   We
live in an age which is protesting so vehemently
against false sentiment that expression in all the
arts has become strident and insolent.   The
Manchester Guardian writer applauds the *Domestic
Symphony* of Strauss because it dares to speak of
earthly things in a human and suburban way.
And, I imagine, he would equally applaud the
younger men (say, Poulenc, Auric, Milhaud and
the rest) for their elaborate and expensive fun.
Even Ravel and Debussy, because they have
cared for the intangible things and for elegant
expression, have already become back numbers
to give room for these dare-devils.   On every
side we hear works of music being praised and
advocated because of some new vaulting ambition
—because of what they have attempted to

express, hardly ever because of the success of the venture.

The desire to formulate the language of music so that it can be compiled in a kind of dictionary is as wrong-headed as it is futile. When we hear the chord of the ninth defined as ' any Tristan making love to any Isolde ', we may suspect an overstrained sense of humour. A word calls up an image through long association and through a crying human need ; there is nothing arbitrary in the connexion between the thing ' egg ' and the word ' egg ' ; but what is this wild notion of chaining (even in jest) a chord or a whole phrase to a definite image or sensation ? Music is as free as the air—' the sounding air ' which is its material. Mr. Binyon suggested that expression in music is less conditioned by material than in the other arts. It would be more nearly true to say that musical expression is less dependent than the other arts upon the laws of association. Music is conditioned by its material as fully and literally as poetry, but whereas poetry uses the most direct vehicle of human intercourse, music uses a more remote and extensive medium. There may be room for a greater liberty in employ-ing this medium, but there is also room for a greater licence ; and in this we may find one of the many reasons why it is more difficult to give a final judgement upon a musical than upon a poetic composition.

Criticism, whether of music or poetry, seeks

first of all for motive. The motive for poetic utterance, however obscured it may be by mannerism, philosophic irrelevance, fantasy or arabesque, is comparatively easy to discover ; but in music not only is it less tangible but often quite incomprehensible to certain types of contemporary criticism. It is not reasonable, for instance, to expect English critics to appraise the work of Schönberg, whose motives are so hedged round about by his own problematic personality. And it is because the material of music is so nebulous that the conditioning of music is so limitless and so exposed to vandalism. In the midst of the vast endless sea of musical expression the only hope is to throw out the anchor of innocence and recover that blessed state of mind which Yeats has described as ' all knowledge lost in trance of sweeter ignorance '.

BEETHOVEN CRITICISM

SO much was written on the subject of Beethoven during the centenary that it became almost impossible to summarize the evidence. After reading various appraisements of the symphonies, concertos, sonatas, quartets, songs, etc., we found ourselves in the position of a man who knows more than he can conveniently remember. But whatever the specializing critics had and may have to say, the fact remains that Beethoven as a composer is looked upon with a great deal of misgiving by the younger generation of the musical public. There is no composer who divides the camps so effectively. On the one hand we meet with the eloquent and forceful poetic utterance of Mr. W. J. Turner, who holds that ' in the music of Beethoven there are no anodynes, no lullings of the sense, no deceits of the intelligence, but pure *virtus* ' ; on the other hand we hear the taunts of the bold unbiddable children of the new age. On this side Sir Henry Hadow assures us that ' Beethoven had the greatest constructive genius of any musician who ever lived—perhaps of any artist except Shakespeare ' ; on the other, we find those who are only too willing to accept Wurzer's early impression that Beethoven was

4 49

stupid and dull. Both these criticisms cannot be true at the same time. On the other hand it is quite possible for both to be in the wrong. The intensive culture of Beethoven's music such as took place all over Europe during the centenary celebrations will do little in the way of proselytizing. Those who believed already were confirmed in their faith ; those who called themselves heretics gloried the more in their excommunication.

It is possible, however, and even likely that the centenary will lead to the development of a middle party—a group consisting of those who consider that Beethoven wrote great and fine music, but who do not consider that Thayer's biography is an irreverent assault upon a sacred stronghold. It is to this group that we look for the real Beethoven criticism, for these are the people who will not allow their judgement to be deflected either by oppressive piety or by rebellious zeal. They are not afraid to acknowledge the versatility of expression revealed in the Rasoumovsky Quartets ; at the same time they do not count themselves Philistines for preferring the best of Mozart's quartet-writing to the Opus 18 Quartets. Freely they admit the immensity of conception and the structural strength embodied in the greatest of the sonatas and symphonies ; and admitting these things, they claim the right to point to other works in which the conception is obscured and the structure full of flaws. They have the prudence to realize that if Beethoven is unreasonably idolized by this generation, the next will most surely become iconoclastic. That is the way of the world in every sphere of activity. The reaction against the ' verbal inspiration ' school of theology led to the most preposterous claims on the part of the scientists. The reign of the Puritans in England was followed by a lamentably one-sided cultivation of the arts. The Victorian habit of lionizing, garlanding, and haloing prominent public figures has brought about this present age of insolence and excessive publication.

In the same way, if the Beethoven centenary leads to anything but a true and just valuation of the composer's influence and attainment, if there is any deliberate or accidental misrepresentation as to the extent of his appeal, then, just as surely as night follows day, there will ensue a period during which the works of Beethoven will be shamefully neglected and his fame will be looked upon as an artificial product of early twentieth-century commercialism. For nobody can deny that the centenary celebrations could never have been carried out on so wide a basis but for the co-operation, and in some cases the initiation of the Press, broadcasting, the gramophone companies and the publishing firms. Our little motives and systems are so magnified by the amplifying processes of commercial concern that we are constantly being encouraged to strike an attitude of pride and self-congratulation. Man is no bigger than he was ; but his deeds often assume an importance out of all proportion with their origin. Let him but say ' I think so ' or ' Certainly not ', and his words are blown about the four corners of the earth. Pity him then for his conceit. Pity him if he uses some of the reflected glory of a man like Beethoven in order that his own breast shall gleam a little.

There is one form of Beethoven criticism in particular against which we must guard. It is the kind that commonly professes awe in the face of works which are incomprehensible. Here is one example : ' Even when that expression is obscure, there is always the consciousness that the dark places are in the mind of the hearer, not in the brain of the maker.' And here is another : ' Like the drawings of Blake, these (the posthumous) quartets seem to be striving to give coherence to things which can only dwell in the creator's imagination as a nebulous and formless vision. Perhaps they may be regarded as sketches for larger works too idealistic to be capable of actual realization. . . . The last quartets were so full of intimate questionings that they were sometimes almost inarticulate, if one can describe music in such a way.'

The fact is, of course, that one *cannot* describe music in such a way. Music which does not articulate is no longer music. Things which can only dwell in the creator's imagination as

' a formless vision ' are excluded from musical
content by definition ; for that which is without
form is also void so far as expression is concerned.
Critics are very fond of excusing Beethoven in
this way. Had he been a composer of less
renown and greatness, his last quartets would
have been criticized more fairly and squarely.
The fact that even after a hundred years we are
still unable to follow their metaphysical import,
or even to comprehend their speech at times,
gives us good ground to suspect that in these
works at least Beethoven failed in his high
endeavour.

Sir Alexander Mackenzie has told us that the
only way to approach these works is ' with
reverence '. With all due respect, to approach
them with an open and enlightened mind seems
to be a far better way. In any case we do no
honour to a composer merely by bowing our
heads and faintly murmuring, ' Alas ! This
music means nothing to me '. Shakespeare is
not honoured by the assertion that *Titus
Andronicus* is a good play. Neither is Beethoven
extolled by the statement that in the posthumous
quartets he was struggling to encompass that
which is beyond the length and breadth and depth
of man's thoughts.

Let our tribute go to him then, for the might
and the eloquence of his works when he was in
full possession of his powers, not for his
incoherence after the mists had descended

upon his mind. Had he written nothing finer than the F minor Quartet (op. 95) and the B flat Trio (op. 97), his fame would have been assured, and his glory nothing less.

From the vast amount of Beethoven literature published during the early part of 1927 there is in my opinion no more significant statement than this, from Ernest Newman's *The Unconscious Beethoven* : ' Undoubtedly we shape, or fancy we shape, our ideas into the forms we desire ; but as undoubtedly the ideas have a life of their own.' This represents the whole of Beethoven criticism reduced to a simple but profound statement. The context of the sentence is an admirably clear discussion of the subconscious and unconscious processes which were continually directing the creative power of Beethoven. ' How far is genius conscious of itself ? ' is the question Mr. Newman raises, and so far as Beethoven is concerned, he gives this answer : ' That obsession (the persistence of the three-note figure) is perhaps the most remarkable of the many features of Beethoven's style that tempt us to think of him as the unconscious medium through which a musical idea worked, rather than as the conscious discoverer and manipulator of the idea.' This is a conclusion which demands an answer to a further question before it can be finally established. That question is : How far are we justified in dividing the conscious, subconscious, and unconscious into three water-tight, or, if not water-tight, distinct departments ? Elsewhere in his book Mr. Newman criticizes Schindler and Lenz for being more concerned with the difference between Beethoven's three styles than with the unity underlying them. We may make a parallel criticism and say that in every artist there is not only a conjunction but an essential unity of the conscious, subconscious, and unconscious. And if this is so we are fully justified in regarding the unconscious working of an idea as being only another aspect—the reverse aspect, if you will— of the conscious discovery of that idea. Beethoven is a unique instance of the merging and inter-penetration of these three elements. There can be no more eloquent proof of this than Notte-bohm's 'Four Great Sketches' of the Eroica. From Mr. Newman's lucid exposition of these we may quite legitimately conclude that, with Beethoven, Vision, Inspiration, and Technique— the three elements essential to creation—are practically the same process. Let me repeat the definitions I gave in the last essay. Vision is the orderliness of the artist's experience. Inspiration is the orderliness of his thought and purpose. Technique is the orderliness of his work. Beethoven's striving was almost wholly concerned with the establishment of law and order—the elimination of irrelevancy, the quelling of turbulence, and the refining of conception.

In his book *Beethoven, the Search for Reality* Mr. W. J. Turner has expressed the same idea in this way : ' Creation of any sort implies rejection because it imposes a form upon chaos ', and again : ' A work of art is simply organized experience ', and in the term ' experience ' Mr. Turner includes what he calls ' subjective vision '. The trouble is that later on he almost denies that the *Credo* in Bach's B minor Mass is a work of art, by asserting that there is ' no belief there, not the slightest ; no, nor any imagination either '. It is this kind of violence which damages the effect of Mr. Turner's research magnificent. He is not content with a positive and absolute analysis of Beethoven's creative force ; he must needs arrange an ascending scale in which Bach, Wagner, Mozart, and Beethoven are successive steps. In order to make everything of the Mass in D, it is necessary for him to make nothing of the Mass in B minor, and although he defends the comparative method with a taunt, he does not make it less odious by likening Wagner to a bull and Bach to an ox.

Yet, in spite of the occasional roughness of his methods, Mr. Turner, through sheer courage and intensity of thought, often steps on to high ground. His highest achievement culminates in the following passages : ' But in my opinion there has never been before or since in the history of art so tremendous and so sustained an effort to go so far, to discover so much, and to impose so comprehensive an order upon all that was found in that journey, nor so firm a determination not to surrender a single object.' And again : ' It is Beethoven's supreme quality that not only did he refuse to cheat himself with a pretentious and insincere ritual (such as *Parsifal*), pretending that he himself had made a sacrifice by a show, a spectacle of sacrifice—there being no real victim ; but more than that, he actually sacrificed less than anybody and up to his last day persisted in his refusal to give up one jot of his human experience or in any way to agree with himself to limit it.'

In this last sentence we find Beethoven's eternal dilemma disclosed. Both his strength and his weakness lay in the fact that the whole of his experience was directed through the stream of musical expression. The existing river-beds were often too shallow to hold the fulness of that flood, and constantly we find—especially towards the end of his life—that the banks have been broken, and that the river, in finding its way out to the sea, has made for itself an elaborate delta. It never occurred to Beethoven that he might check and control the flow of this mighty river by building a series of reservoirs upstream, nor was he even aware that the clarity of these rushing waters was often bemired by the admission of experience which could not be conveyed through the medium of music. I have already objected to the kind of criticism which extols the posthumous quartets because they are often inarticulate. The stammer and impediment in these works can only be explained by the presence of extra-musical experience, and the more often one encounters their courageous adventures the more one is convinced that Beethoven was sublimating his inner consciousness so finely and perfectly that the splendid agonizing struggles of his spirit would ultimately have found expression in a rich and wondrous silence. Silence is not the negation but the only true resolution and fulfilment of the music of the universe. It is the greatest of all music, because it contains the whole of music. And nothing less than Silence—the awareness of all music—would have been high and wide and deep enough to hold the solitude and ' perpetual distance ' of Beethoven's inner life.

THE TYRANNY OF THE PERFORMER

THERE have been many signs of late that the head that wears the crown of criticism is lying a little uneasily. At a recent annual dinner of the Critics' Circle, various speeches were made which seemed to indicate that criticism was no more than a tolerated guest of the Arts, and tolerated only on the condition of good behaviour. The alarming thing was that this attitude was assumed chiefly by the critics themselves. They all gave the impression that they were eternally and profoundly grateful for being allowed to sustain themselves on the crumbs which are continually falling from the high altar of the priestly performer. Mr. St. John Ervine likened the critics to parasites, and, later on, to wolves; Mr. E. A. Baughan lisped the prettiest compliments to various actresses who happened to be sitting near him; Mr. H. C. Colles let out a secret which, had it not been an open one, might have wounded the pride of his musical fraternity; and, most shattering of all, Dr. Vaughan Williams gave out that the composer was nothing without his interpreter, and spoke lightly of the composer's work as 'putting down so many black dots on paper'. Now I am fully aware that these speeches were delivered under the rosy cloud of after-dinner gaiety, and that next morning the speakers remembered all the points which they intended to make, and the lines they intended to take. Even so, the fact that the words were uttered in the presence of Press reporters and, more important still, in the hearing of a representative body of dramatic and musical performers, has caused me to protest with all the vehemence I can summon against their implication. For these speakers implied what is most false and most deadly—that is, that the interpreter is the be-all and end-all of all artistic creation, and that the creator himself is a worm and no man. It is an implication which is typical of an age when to perform is considered more honourable than to conceive. (We have only to remind ourselves of woman's emancipation to realize how typical it is.) But, even if typical, how entirely perverse! Those who have refused to be ground down by the tyranny of custom, and have refused to stunt their mental growth by resorting to the drudgery of fashion, know full well that the interpreter, and not the critic, is the guest of Art; he is given the use of certain rooms in the house, and, if he is a true-born gentleman, he will know his proper duty towards his host.

But the trouble is that there are so few gentlemen among our performers to-day. Pray do not mistake me for a snob! I am referring not to social but to spiritual behaviour! There is surely

nobody who would seriously deny that contemporary actors, singers, conductors, etc., exist
entirely by reason of their talent for exploiting the
fixed and known quantities of the greatest works
of art. Time was when *Hamlet* and Beethoven's
symphonies and Schubert's songs existed in their
own right. But do they so now ? Is it not
more true to say that *Hamlet* exists by no right of
its own, but by kind permission of John Barrymore
or Sir Barry Jackson ? (Sir Barry was a prudent
landlord, you remember, and split up the Elsinore
Castle into up-to-date flats with central heating.)
Is it not more true to say that Beethoven's
symphonies must pay homage to the wooden
sceptre of ' you know who I mean ', and that
Schubert's songs must acknowledge the courtesy
of that very specialized autocrat ' the Lieder-
singer ' ? Of course, contemporary composers,
dramatists, and critics favour, or pretend to
favour, this usurpation. There is nothing else
for them to do ; they have been caught up in
the relentless machinery of a commercial age.
There was one speech at this dinner which sounded
the note of truth. Mr. Sean O'Casey has not been
the ' lion in a den of Daniels ' for so long that he
has lost his primitive and just sense of values.
He had the vision, therefore, and the courage to
declare that the play, and not the dramatist or the
actor, was by far the most important element in
the theatre ; and this before quite a number of
people who had hypnotized themselves into the

easy belief that the existence of the theatre is coincidental with their own ! I was especially glad to hear this from Mr. O'Casey. He, at least, did not fall into that dangerous habit of mind which Lord Acton described as ' the sanctification of success '.

At another meeting of the Critics' Circle, the subject of ' The Place of the Actor in Criticism ' was discussed at great length. Many varying opinions were expressed, but none more vigorously than those of Mr. Sydney Carroll. His views were violently opposed to those of Mr. O'Casey, and it was his speech which was chiefly responsible for creating the final impression that the play and the players were equally important and should be given equal prominence in critical accounts. Thereby the present practice of allotting a few reluctant lines to an appraisement of the acting was condemned as being ungenerous and ill-balanced. You may consider it odd that critics should thus criticize their own habits ; if so, you forget that the critics of the daily papers, and those of the weeklies too, must always bow in the journalistic house of Rimmon, and since editors make use of play-productions chiefly, and often merely, for their news-value, the critic's first duty is to tell his readers what the play is about, or, at any rate, what it is like. Having done this, he usually finds that he has all but outrun the confines of time and space, and so, by way of postscript (as many critics confessed at this discussion), indulges in a little display of adjectival juggling.

To many this custom may seem grossly unjust to the actor. My own opinion is that it is as it should be, and my reasons are not editorial but strictly personal. During the last ten years or so it has become apparent that dramatic critics have submitted—unwittingly, perhaps, in some cases—to the growing tyranny of the players. The servility of intelligence is a painful thing to observe, and it is because I have observed it that I now protest with as much intensity as is seemly. During this meeting there were no actual confessions of this weakness, but throughout there were undercurrents and implications which gave colour to what had formerly been my suspicions. The various speakers let fall such phrases as ' When the actors read the criticism next morning . . .', ' We ought to see to it that the players get their due share in the success of a play ', ' It is difficult sometimes to let off a star-performer lightly ', etc. These phrases reveal the trend of journalistic criticism. It is far too much concerned with ' personalities ', reputations, principalities and powers—far too agitated about the welfare of charming actresses, far too much concerned with irrelevance. Dramatic critics (and maybe the other critics too, but I am not concerned with them here) have in many cases fallen to the ranks of Press-agents. They spend their time making ' selections ' after the manner of racing correspondents. Their vanity is gratified by nothing so much as the appearance of a theatre poster bearing a quotation from one of their notices, ' " I predict a great future for this young actress." —X. Y. in the ——, March 16th, 1928.' Theatre managers and Press representatives are aware of this little weakness, and are constantly luring the critic on with the prospect of cheap and wide publicity, so much so that glaringly bad productions are constantly being given the hall-mark of a critic's initials.

It would be interesting to discover the real origin of the current complaint that the players are being neglected by dramatic criticism. I think there would not be much difficulty in tracing it back to the players themselves. Actors are notoriously avaricious where publicity is concerned, and in spite of the fact that they are more freely advertised than any other class of professional, they consent to the most obviously illegitimate forms of advertising enterprise (the documented approval of a vanishing cream or a razor blade, for example) in order to persuade the credulous public of their histrionic powers. They submit to a foolish, unentertaining cross-examination as to their highest attainment of mystical experience and the food they like best to eat, and answer the questions with a laborious air of gaiety. Success, for them, is measured numerically by newspaper paragraphs.

Max Beerbohm bids us ponder the formula,

' The actor's medium is himself.' It is so much a formula that its full significance is difficult to capture. A man who carries on his profession in the continuous presence of an impressionable and garrulous populace can scarcely be said to have a grievance against a critic who concentrates his faculties upon forming and delivering a judgement upon a work of the dramatic art. For Max Beerbohm's formula follows as a corollary from another which is this, ' The play's medium is the player ', so that in any criticism of a play-production there is always implied and contained a further criticism of the quality of its presentation, which is a smaller concentric circle within the larger one. A well-balanced and just account of the immediate effect of a play will, as a matter of course, convey the relative value of the acting, and if the players complain that this is too anonymous a method for the aggrandizement of their box-office value, they are answered at once by the first axiom of the theatre, which is that anonymity is one of the surest aids to illusion. The insistence upon static and formulated personality explains the fact that, except in theory, there is no such thing as the English Theatre.

When we say that the play's medium is the player, we include, of course, the producer in our consideration, for the producer's medium is also the player. At the discussion to which I have referred, a few speakers professed to find an insoluble problem in the growing prominence of

5

the producer. Mr. Percy Allen, with a baffled, unhappy expression upon his face, asked, ' When I find a performance (in a play I have read or seen before) wholly at variance with my preconception of the character, am I to pillory the actor or the producer ? ' Mr. Allen had previously told us that he had severely criticized the two leading players in a recent Ibsen revival for their complete misunderstanding of the philosophical idea behind the play. Afterwards he discovered that the interpretation had been forced upon the players against their own judgement by the producer. But I think Mr. Allen had taken his error too much to heart. Indeed, it can fairly be said that it was no error at all, since it is definitely no business of the critic to know what happens at rehearsals and behind the scenes. He is invited to a first performance, and from that fact he may safely assume that he is asked to give judgement upon what he experiences there and then, without any reference whatsoever to the domestic differences of the company. If those differences have existed during rehearsals the critic's attitude should be, ' What have I to do with them ? If an actor disagrees with his producer, and feels that he cannot recreate the producer's ideas, it is open to him to resign the part. After all, the actor's is the stronger case, for the first thing I look for in a producer is the talent for casting a play. When, therefore, I see the announcement that a certain actor will play Iago, and that the play will be produced by Basil Dean, I cannot be expected to know more than this—that Mr. Dean has formed his own ideas about the character of Iago, and that he is satisfied that the actor he has chosen will concur (either actively or passively) with those ideas.'

This may be cold comfort for Mr. Allen's sensitive conscience, but in my own opinion he was perfectly justified in ignoring the fact that the players were very likely only too eager to give him the interpretation he wanted, but had been overwhelmed and stifled by a tyrannous overlord. In any case, I beg him not to create the precedent of attending rehearsals in order to be quite sure that he knows the facts of the case. His last state of mind would then be worse than the first!

.   .   .   .   .

The ' performer ' is so hedged round about by sacerdotal observances that he cannot possibly understand the anomaly of his position. These words of mine, zealous though they be, will fall vainly upon his ear. But there is a faint hope that the oddly mysterious entity which we call by the blunt name of ' the public ' will hear and understand this final utterance : In the beginning was the critical word ; creation followed as a matter of course. Performance was not called in until the creative instinct was exhausted ; and, lastly, when the performing instinct was threatened with extinction, it was kept alive by the artificial means of professionalism.

How inverted are the minds of those critics who smite their breasts at the Temple entrance and whisper about their own unworthiness ! Do they not know that they have, and rightly have, plenary powers over the mere performer ? For without criticism, nothing is.

THE COOL MUSIC OF HASLEMERE

IN one of her letters Mme. de Charrière let fall the remark : ' I find occupations which depend on nobody but myself, and get amusement enough in my own way.' Arnold Dolmetsch could say the same with a little qualification. Of course his music-making depends in great measure upon the gifted members of his family, and on some occasions upon his disciples, but, in spite of this, there is perhaps no musician of the present time who is more self-dependent and self-sufficient than Dolmetsch. The festivals of old chamber music which are given at Haslemere each year, prove his courage and his conviction, and there are signs that the vigour of his faith is compelling more and more people to revise their easy preconceptions as to the true nature of music. You cannot be brought into the presence of this music of the ' golden age ' without realizing how great a gulf is fixed between it and that unknown quantity which is called ' modern music '.

Arnold Dolmetsch is a man of dominating purpose, a man of passionate beliefs. It is often to be noted that whenever a man decides to make research in a period of history neglected by the majority, he is inclined to lose a proper perspective, and to become freakish and absurd. There are some, I know, who look upon Dolmetsch as a picturesque fanatic. They betray a superficial knowledge of the man. It is impossible to talk with him (or rather, to hear him propound) for more than a few minutes without becoming conscious of the unusual force of his faith. Of course, it seems fanatical for a man to stand up and declare to this idolatrous and professional generation that applause at a concert is heretical —that indeed, the whole idea of concert-giving is antithetical to the true spirit of music—that music-making in the home is the ultimate ideal. But the fanaticism begins to reflect the colour of good sound sense when we find that the man who is so vehement in his speech is also zealous in his works. The faith of Dolmetsch, made real and visible as it is in his own handicraft, and that of his family in Jesses workshop, becomes a thing of splendour and inspiration. And perhaps the greatest tribute to the influence of his thought and labour is the devotion of his disciples. They are few as yet, but already they give proof that the leaven is working. Some years ago in Liverpool a few musicians began to study the viols and viol-playing, and now similar consort-ings are being made in other centres.

Maybe none of us will live to see the complete renascence of the amateur spirit in music, but surely there are few who will deny that that spirit is above all things most desirable. Where is the critic to-day who can truly and fearlessly write of his best-beloved works of music that they have been to himself ' as Divine Raptures, Powerfully Captivating all unruly Faculties and Affections (for the Time) ', and disposing him ' to Solidity, Gravity, and a good Temper ' ? Yet Thomas Mace could so write of the music of his time—and without a trace of self-consciousness.

To realize the extreme fineness of the work of these English writers it is necessary to hear their works over and over again, until the elusive idiom of their musical thought is securely captured. I well remember hearing a performance of William Lawes ' *Fantasy and Aire* for six viols in G minor. This to me is one of the most interesting works of the period. It is typical of the fund of beauty and resource which this school possessed.

William Lawes, who hitherto has been known to most of us only through his songs, was but one in a large and glorious company. The music of Thomas Tomkins, John Jenkins (whose *First Fantasy* is full of the most surprising inventions), Michael Easte, and Richard Deering leads us to look upon the texture of present-day music from a new standpoint. Roger North, who was a pupil of John Jenkins, wrote of the English fantasy : ' It is not like a hurry of action, as looking on at a battle where the concern for the one side or the other makes a pleasure.'

His words are curiously prophetic in a negative way, for contemporary musical activity is like nothing so much as a ' hurry of action '. And, of course, this is inevitable, seeing that musical creation always reflects the conditions of its environment. Yet it is good at times to return to the music of ' cool air ' and ' temperate summer evenings '; at Haslemere, we can sometimes fall back upon the amplitude and self-possession of the fantasy writers and forget that the world has moved since the year 1700.

Not many years ago Parry wrote these words : ' There is hardly any nation worse supplied with music which represents its true characteristics than the English.' There is only one conclusion to draw from this statement, and that is, that Parry, authority as he was in some respects, had very little direct experience of the viol music which was being written by English composers of this period. For there is no music, before or since, which so faithfully reflects the English temperament.

And how encouraging it is to discover that these sixteenth- and seventeenth-century English musicians could write genuine instrumental music ! —music, too, which always presents a united front (aided by the perfect blending of the viols) for all the seeming self-determination of the counterpoint. There is no attempt to break the bounds of seemliness, no vehemence, no steep gradients in the melodic lines, no violence or passion in the rhythmic flow. And yet to hear this music in the context of the other European schools of the time is to be convinced of the superiority of the English. Maybe their own peculiar form of rhythmic impulse is considered by some to be tame and unenterprising, compared with the vivacity of the Southern Europeans ; but it is easy to demonstrate that this view is based upon an entirely false idea of what rhythm really is. For there is insistent rhythm and there is implied rhythm. The viols are never allowed to protest by the English writers. Theirs is the art of gentle implication. Their linear thought implies harmonic thought, and, indeed, creates it ; and, in like manner, their harmonic thought implies and begets rhythm.

These English writers of concerted viol music often made use of a simple four-note theme, consisting of the tonic, second, fourth and third of the scale. It was the common practice of the time to take a theme with some holy association as a kind of invocation for inspiration. This accounts for a great number of works bearing the title ' In Nomine '. At first they were founded upon a theme from the Gregorian liturgy, but in later works bearing the same title it is difficult to discover the actual theme, although the atmosphere is always appropriate in its austerity. The word ' theme ' in this connexion does not contain the significance which it has in the later sonatas. The fantasy themes are not set up against each other for contrast of rhythm, mood or tonality ; they are merely threads, and their function is to appear and reappear in the woven

texture until the pattern is complete. The
repetitions are sometimes literal, sometimes in
double or triple time, sometimes in inversion,
sometimes diminished, and sometimes augmented.
There is no striving among the instruments for
mastery ; the effect is obtained by skilful interplay rather than by opposition. Those who
assert that the fantasy lacks form and direction
are thereby confessing their own lack of perception. They are judging this early music by later
standards and conformities. It is the poorest
kind of criticism which can see no beauty in a
violet because it does not embody the more
aspiring qualities of a sunflower. Ferrabosco's
Four-Note Pavan (for five viols) does not proclaim
its form in any outside show. We cannot analyse
it so as to point here to first and there to second
subjects, here to exposition and development,
and there to recapitulation, but for all that,
the form is there, lending unity and coherence to
the sounds and giving them a wonderful self-
sufficiency. And the same can be said of Morley's
Il Doloroso for two viols (a perfect instrumental
marriage), and of Richard Deering's ethereal
Fantasy in C.

The festivals have been remarkable for many
things, but none more important than a performance in 1926 of the *Fourth Brandenburg Concerto*
(in G major) in its original form ; that is to say,
with solo violin and recorders in G. This was
probably the first time an English audience had

heard the work in that form. The previous year Dolmetsch was compelled to give the work in Bach's later arrangement (in which the violin part was given over to the harpsichord), because he had no G recorders (echo flutes, as Bach called them). But, fired with the desire to give the work ' in native worth ', he applied himself to the production of two of these instruments at his workshop. At length they were constructed, and their soft beguiling voices can once more be heard in the land. Immediately it became clear why they were called echo flutes, for in the lovely *andante* movement there are repeated phrases which can be played softly on each second occasion without altering the pitch.

The music of Bach occupies an important place in the programme-schemes drawn up each year. There is significance in this. We are all thoroughly accustomed just now to what is generally known as a Bach ' revival '. Indeed, the danger seems to be that the revival will be carried too far and will cause a serious reaction. Only the other day I heard a well-known and eminent English composer declare that to him Bach's last movements were like the relentless workings of a sewing machine. That opinion may or may not have been bluff, but it gives us our cue. Arnold Dolmetsch gives Bach a place of especial prominence in his festivals not because he is intent upon a wholesale revival of Bach's music, but because to him Bach represents the culmination

of all the glorious adventures of European music*
during the sixteenth and seventeenth centuries.
His advent marks the climax of the Research
Magnificent. Too often we look upon Bach as a
lonely, mighty figure, having no relation to his
contemporaries and immediate predecessors. We
single him out as if contrapuntal writing were a
thing unknown before he came, or, if not unknown,
at least too crude to be graced with the name of
composition.

Sebastian Bach, so far from being isolated, is
in the very centre of the genealogical table of
musical creation. Indeed, he was the summary
of all that had gone before. He was the justification for the many experiments in musical form
which had been made during the seventeenth
century. He took the early essays in sonata form,
indefinite as they often were, and gave them
feature, and not only feature but expression and
the fulness of life. He was ' bringer of truth out
of the hidden '.

After the recovery of the G recorders, Dolmetsch proceeded to bring back the other missing
members of the recorder family, until at length a
full consort was possible—descant, two trebles,
tenor and bass. These have been heard together
in popular tunes of the sixteenth and seventeenth
centuries. It is an interesting fact that Purcell

---

*Always excepting, of course, the English school, which
came to an unnatural and shameful end after the middle of
the seventeenth century.

often wrote for a combination of three recorders. His *Chaconne* called *Two in One upon a Ground* is a wonderful interplay of rounded tones. This work served to bring forward a newly-constructed bass recorder for its first public appearance. The quality of its voice was sustaining without any of the aggression usually associated with foundation tones.

Compared with the English composers of the seventeenth century, much of the French music of the period appears to be merely decorative. Henri Dumont, Master of Music to Henri Quatre, and Marin Marais were among the few French composers of the time who occasionally struck a note of austerity and high-mindedness. It was left, however, to Couperin and Rameau to show that French music could be concerned with other things than manner and style. Such a movement as *Le Moucheron*, for example, reveals not only fine workmanship but also the substance of genuine musical thought. These men at least did not write music as one might attempt to solve a quadratic equation. Music was for them a way of expressing an inner consciousness, and not merely an attempt to overcome a series of obstacles.

As for the Italians of this period, they were rarely anything more than good stylists. This is not to applaud all the romantics and ‘ cry them for the mode ’. Style was an important element at a time when musical creation was prone to be indefinite and aimlessly experimental. As an

instance, Frescobaldi's fantasia upon the old tune
La Bergamasca, for four viols, is an interesting
experiment in variation form, but it leaves the
impression of being too much concerned with the
safe anchorage of the tune, and so fails to obtain
any clearly-marked contrasts in the movements ;
and a whole concert of early Italian music leaves
me with a disconcerting sense of loneliness, as if
I had been shown into a large and airy room with
a beautifully polished floor, had been invited to
take a seat and make myself at home, and then
had failed to find a single piece of furniture upon
which I could sit, lean or recline.

   .   .   .   .   .

One of the most vivid of my Haslemere
memories is of an occasion when Dolmetsch came
forward and announced that he would play the
Bach *Chaconne* for unaccompanied violin.   First
of all, he decried the eternal performance of this
work by present-day violinists, who suffer under
the delusion that no recital programme is considered genuine until it has been stamped with
the hall-mark of this composition.   He declared
that it was impossible for them to give anything
like a faithful version of the music on a modern
violin.   Three- and four-note chords, for instance,
had to be played in *arpeggio* fashion because the
strings of the later instruments are arranged in
such a way that they cannot all be stroked by

the bow at the same time. The older violin, an example of which Dolmetsch used for this performance, was fashioned so that on necessary occasions its strings could, so to speak, be entirely enclosed by the bow. There was also a difference in the construction of the bow which made this possible.

Dolmetsch prayed for good luck in his first public performance of the work, and at the end confessed that a fair measure of fortune had attended him. The chord passages were certainly much firmer and fuller in relation to the tone of the context than in the recital performances to which hitherto I had been accustomed. Moreover, Dolmetsch from time to time employed devices, well known to the violinists of Bach's time, which had the effect of deflecting the string quality, and giving it a wood-wind effect, sometimes flute and sometimes reed. After the concert I heard a good deal of controversy over the performance. To those who are acquainted with the history of stringed instruments, there can be no surprise that there should be this dissent. It has ever been thus with the violin. At the beginning it was regarded as an impostor—a disturber of the domestic peace of the viols. We learn from Anthony Wood that before the Restoration, gentlemen—that is to say, real gentlemen—always preferred viols, ' for they esteemed a violin to be an instrument only belonging to a common fiddler, and could

not endure that it should come among them, for
feare of making their meetings to be vaine and
fidling '. Thomas Mace, whose predilection was
for the music of the better days that were gone,
spoke of these instruments as ' scoulding Violins ',
and of their tone quality he gives the opinion that
when they ' run over some Coranto, Sarabande,
or Brawle, or such-like stuff, they be fit to make a
Man's Ears Glow, and to fill his brains full of
Friskes, etc., than to season and Sober his Mind,
or Elevate his Affections to Goodness '.

The instrument nearest to Dolmetsch's heart
is the clavichord. Whenever he plays upon it he
invites his audience to gather around him, for the
purpose of creating a greater intimacy with the
music. Once I heard him play the Prelude and
Fugue in D minor from Book I of the *Forty-
eight*. It seemed that he had captured the music
which exists beyond all sense and aural perception.
For a brief moment the world was hushed, and
over and above the hush a new sound was heard—
a strange, gentle sound that gave echo to things
once intimate and now sadly out-of-mind.

PIANOLA: OR THE FUTURE OF MUSIC-MAKING

I

NO unusual gift of discernment is needed in order to be aware that the conditions of musical performance are suffering a change at the present time. It is not for me to say that the change is for better or for worse. That is beside the point, and in any case it is impossible to pass any such judgement until the process has brought us to some definite point of review. We have not yet arrived at any such point, and in spite of the speed of the voyage it is not likely that we shall be able to disembark for some time to come. Nevertheless it is possible to observe from time to time, in a more or less detached frame of mind, various characteristics and features that may be taken as reliable evidence. The first thing that is apparent, even to the most superficial observer, is that there are far too many people who profess themselves musical performers. Their numbers are too good to be true. A student of singing learns a score of songs, and immediately takes steps to hire a concert hall in which to sing them to an audience of admiring friends and vainglorious relations.

The agents, having no conscience in this matter, invite the critics to attend, just as they invite them to attend a recital by Gerhardt or John McCormack. They make no distinction. The result is that the critic finds it necessary to work upon a delicately measured *rubato* basis. He robs Heifetz to pay some half-fledged beginner who ' promises well '. There is a definite danger here. The enormous influence of the advertisement-fed Press reacts perniciously upon criticism. Because certain recitals are advertised in a given newspaper, the critic of that journal finds himself in the ignominious position of a supervisor of studies. Let him be never so alert and wary, he is always in danger of losing that fineness of perception which is his either by achievement or by right divine. His continual attention to asthmatic tone and invertebrate phrasing must needs in the end induce a kind of sympathy with infirmity, however unconscious the sympathy may be. For he must consider not only the welfare of music, but also the welfare of the proprietors of his journal. He must also consider the law of libel.

We see then that performance is becoming less and less professional. This applies to drama, and (with modification) to literature and painting, as well as to music. The corollary of this is that audiences and performers are fast becomng a community. Singers attend song recitals, actors give up their only free evening to see an ill-prepared production by a Sunday society, authors travel far to see new plays by their contemporaries. Recently the view was expressed that the fine arts will soon become, like hunting, ' the symbol of an idle and strictly useless life '. While we may admit that the lives of the majority of singers and players are strictly useless, it is only too evident that they are not idle ; moreover, their numbers and activities are steadily increasing. But the increase, so far from producing rich attainment, appears to be the cause of its impoverishment. Two reasons for this reaction can be singled out from others not so important or obvious.

In the first place the economic conditions of present-day musical life provide an *allurement* for would-be performers. It is beside the point of our present consideration that the allurement proves a deception for ninety-five per cent. of these poor souls. With the increasingly complex subdivisions of musical activity, we cannot wonder that the student-singer or instrumentalist is irresistibly drawn into the relentless machinery of it all. ' If I fail at this, I can try that.' A cruel illusion, but who can dispel its influence ? The lure is so effective that the single- and half-talents enter the competition with the fives and tens. Even the no-talents are only too willing to take chances, knowing that achievement as a performer is by no means wholly conditioned by purely musical factors. The immediate result of this friction and breathless confusion is that the period of preparation, which in the nature of things should be longer for a musician than for any other kind of artist, is curtailed in order to gain time and a good place in the race. The students are less to blame than their teachers, who are constantly dissipating talent in order to obtain quick returns in the shape of a few perfunctory Press-cuttings.

The second reason has been already implied by the first. The inventions and ingenuities of this century have already caused a change in the nature of musical activity. In the presence of so many machinations and contrivances, musical performance (as an insignificant act) has become so abominably easy. Instinct and refinement are overwhelmed by the rising wave of efficiency. For see what things are possible ! With the aid of a gramophone record, even the intimate and personal elements of interpretation can be closely aped. At a London song recital, I remember hearing a young singer give a faithful reproduction of Chaliapin in ' The Song of the Flea '. As an imitation it was remarkably good (howbeit not salted enough with personal comment to pass in a recital programme), but of the fineness of thought which occasioned the first creation, not a sign could be discovered.

It is clear then that conditions are far too easy (in a superficial sense) to favour a high degree of general competence in the performance of music, and far too commercial to encourage the conjugal rights of Talent and Application.   Talent asserts her wanton inclination to love freely wheresoever she lists, until finally she becomes both unproductive and unprofitable.

.   .   .   .   .

2

For some time past the elaborate organization which is known as the World of Music, has been pressed by an over-eager mediocrity.   It has become the fashion to scorn the influences of the virtuoso, but it is not difficult to see that the fashion is the result of an ignorance as to what the virtuoso really stands for.   He is important not only for utilitarian reasons, not only because he has expanded the ways and means of musical expression, but also because he serves to keep us minded of the magic of performance.   Under the opposite influence of certain schools of composition, we have become too prone to forget that music, unlike the rebuked Victorian child, is meant to be heard and not seen.   The voracity of publishing firms and the slickness of reviewers are gradually obscuring that simple fact.   The prestige of the miniature score reveals that criticism is conditioned almost as much by visual as by audible impressions.   I well remember

hearing a performance of a *Partita* by Paul
Amadeus Pisk, following it with a MS. score. It
so happened that this MS. was most finely and
elegantly copied, a thing of beauty to look upon ;
and I have no doubt that this was an important
factor in the pleasure I received from the performance. During the recent performance of
some pianoforte works by Hindemith, a well-
known authority was heard to remark, ' This
music would sound so much better if we could
follow it with the score.' Here is a dangerous
heresy, and also a significant portent. However
clearly we may perceive its workings, it is well-
nigh impossible to check them, or to counteract
them with an older, wiser, and more natural point
of view. For the heresy is the inevitable result
of the environment of contemporary manners of
thinking. A rough parallel is found in modern
biographical methods, which, as Emil Ludwig
has lucidly pointed out, are much nearer to
the methods of biology than to those of history.
People are so much more interested in cause than
in effect, and would rather see the conflicting
currents at work in the brain of a man like
Bismarck than regard the brain-wave of national
unity which was the objective result of the inner
conflict ; or, to bring the matter home, they
would rather follow the lines of a contrapuntal
score to see how they run, than enjoy the sonorous
projection which was the composer's impulse
and aim.

With conditions such as these, performance tends to become more and more impersonal, and the virtuoso is beginning to lose his singular and essential virtue. By mechanical process the quality of his virtue can be imitated, and even reproduced, so that he finds there is no course open but to enrol himself in the services of the player-piano, or record the erstwhile existence of that virtue upon synthetic wax. And when from time to time the virtuoso appears to us in the flesh, we regard him no more with the eyes of wonder ; we no longer acknowledge his royal descent, his succession by right divine, but think of the limpid flood of his music as being of no more (perhaps of less) consequence than that distilled version which can be turned on at home at any hour of the day. The result appears in various ways, some obvious, others obscure. An obvious result was the half-empty concert hall that one of the greatest living violinists was called upon to face in London a few months ago. It is possible to make objection to this as evidence, to point out that it was a single instance, and that the greatest performers can still be certain of their following. The fact that it *was* a single instance makes it all the more significant, for it revealed the fundamental attitude of the British public towards virtuosity, as soon as the concert agents neglect to appeal to the instincts of self-respect and vanity ; and the evidence, that on most occasions renowned performers continue

to attract large audiences is merely in favour of
the agents' close observation of the laws of
crowd-psychology, and of their adroit application
of those laws.

But even when the concert halls are filled, it
is possible to discern a change in the attitude
towards fine performance, and this change
constitutes what I have called the more obscure
results.   Whenever a great singer or player is
immoderately acclaimed, it is certain that the
impulse has originated in some small, and maybe
dispersed, minority, which usually consists of
aspiring performers. These can know the measure
of the attainment, and knowing it, they see it as
heroic in relation to their own.   They acknowledge the hero, until their enthusiasm leavens the
whole lump.   When this minority is too small
to spread the good news, or when it has been
disappointed in its hero, the lump remains
undisturbed.   In other words, the majority
lacks initiative.   Why ?   Because it also lacks
reverence.   Through the increased activity of
the middle-men of music, ' the terrible robber-
men ', executive genius has become a domestic
article as common as an ash-tray.   Familiarity
has bred, not so much contempt, as indifference.
He would be accounted a strange person who,
before making a call, bowed to his telephone in a
hushed moment of awe and wonder.   And it is
not impossible to imagine a time near at hand
when the expression of any kind of homage in the

presence of a surpassing performance of a musical
work will be considered as a breach of sanity.
This state of affairs is already foreshadowed by
the general tenor of professional criticism. The
reaction from the uncritical adulation or the
equally uncritical invective of the latter half of
the nineteenth century has been so complete that
it is almost impossible to discover a general
official attitude towards any given performer.
Criticism, in the process of becoming more
intensely introspective, is also becoming colour-
less, and, in its preoccupation with a mass of
immediate details, is losing touch with the
ultimate reality. So self-sufficient is the critic
in the fastness of his mind that it would not be
difficult for him, he thinks, to spend the rest of
his days without hearing a single direct performance, and still be able to draw upon the
compound interest of his invested experience.
And with this self-sufficiency, a new note in
criticism can be overheard. It is the jarring note
of insolence. It is struck never so forcibly as
when the critic is brought face to face with the
virtuoso. In the eyes of Criticism (regarded as an
impersonal sum of all critics) there is no longer
any wonder in the subjection of an instrument by
human hands for the re-creation of a fleeting
fantasy of sound. ' He played a sonata well,
badly or indifferently,' and there's an end. We
do not speak of miracles in an age of pitiless
reason.

3

But if we speak not of miracles, nevertheless we harbour, either secretly or shamelessly, an increasing desire to perform them. And the desire is encouraged by the assurance, given on every side, that all things are possible to him who can buy. The performance of these miracles is no longer conditioned, as once it was, by the possession of spiritual insight, since it is no longer a personal performance. They, who have temporal power, can enter into a supernatural world at will, by the movement of a lever or the scratching of a needle. They enter, but do not know it for a supernatural world. To them it is a world of slick organization and clever ideas. They cannot be expected to know the real value of an invention which makes miracles common and almost trivial, for they have been trained to appraise by an unreal system of values based on markets, stocks and shares and dividends. Gramophone companies keep up the pretence that what they are really after is ' the real thing ', and from time to time they announce their progress towards this illusion, and invite the Press to rejoice with them at lunch over that which is being discovered. But a business man will tell you that the progress of a gramophone company is not measured in terms of musical criticism but in terms of hard cash. The reason for this is clear : the new musical public, which is a public given over almost entirely to mediate and conveyed music, is essentially a mercantile public, and in saying this I am using the word ' mercantile ' in its best and not in its offensive sense. The members of that public have been persuaded by the traders of the musical world that for a certain outlay they can enter into that which, hitherto, has been the inheritance of a minority. Their initiation is based upon material endowment and acquirement. No other factor enters into consideration. Naturally, this new power goes to their heads like wine. Their artistic status is seemingly raised. They see themselves as trees walking. And the illusion is encouraged by the mistaken notions of those who seek to pass off the counterfeit currency of information for the sterling worth of understanding.

The inevitable result is that the demands of this mercantile culture are met by an all too eager supply. What are those demands ? We are not surprised to find that they are chiefly concerned with Comfort, Regularity, Efficiency, Speed, and all the qualities which are the chief regard of the *nouveau riche* mentality. (And here it is as well to make clear that this mentality does not necessarily correspond with actual wealth. Indeed, it is much more common than great riches, and is seen at its worst aspect in people who are slightly prosperous.) For these people, music, whether played, replayed or relayed, must first of all be comfortable ; that is to say, it must present no immediate problem, or at least no problem that cannot readily be solved in an analytical note. Secondly, it must be regular ; that is, the supply must be under control. The power of music must be subjected to man's needs, just as water-power, electricity-power and petrol-power are subjected. This leads to the third necessity. Music must be efficient, which means that, at the expense of everything else, it must be literal. This require-ment is met by a number of inventions which give assurance of infallibility so far as note-playing is concerned. How should they, who are waiting to invest, know that a note has no significance in itself ; that even the significance of the note (the sound) is nothing if it is mere sound, unrelated to the conception for which it was called into play ? It is sufficient for them that the notes succeed each other without impediment. At least they serve the purpose of proving that the recipient is not hard of hearing.

Lastly, music must be speedy. The statement has no reference to actual *tempo*. There are examples in sonata music of slow movements that seem to have taken place in a single moment of time, so still and concentrated is their beauty ; and there are examples of final movements that, by reason of their illogical structure or their shortness of breath, give the impression of exceed-ing length and tardiness. When I say that music must necessarily be speedy in order to appeal to the new audience, I mean that it must persuade that audience that no time has been lost ; that is to say, that the time has been well spent, in the literal sense of the phrase. Music and performances that can carry this persuasion at once become popular ; the other kind is discarded as being of no utilitarian value.

These persistent demands, as I have said, are met by a continuous supply, since the existence of any business concern implies dividends, and dividends imply increased output. And for this increase the services of virtuosity, or of what remains of virtuosity, are enlisted. The virtuoso cannot afford to stand aloof and look upon all this activity with disdain. For, if he does not take part in the big push, he knows that his services will very soon be rendered superfluous by ingenious machinations and contrivances. He swallows his pride, therefore, and joins up. After a time, however, he finds that he must change his methods—so much so, that ultimately the very nature of his being is transformed. The virtuoso of old made his appeal not only through his surpassing dexterity but also through the whims of his personality. His performance was an exhibition of polished dare-devilry. But, in tempting Providence, he always did so with a reverent regard. There was no note of mockery in his display. It was rather in the nature of a splendid research which, peradventure, might enrich the resources

of music.   The present-day virtuoso cannot hope
to enrich those resources in the face of the endowment of scientific discovery.   He therefore cancels
the more personal element of his performance,
and emphasizes the purely mechanical side, hoping
thereby to retain at least a moiety of his former
popularity.   In spite of his courage and extreme
efficiency, however, it is already possible to see
that he is playing a losing game, that in time
the Robot Music which he has helped to fabricate
in the shape of piano rolls and gramophone records,
will turn and crush him.

4

We have, then, to face the fact that we have
already begun a new era in the history of music-
making.   It is irrelevant to discuss whether the
prospects are bright or gloomy.   The road has
been taken and the rest of the journey is
inevitable.   Yet, whenever musical societies meet
together, the presidential address is almost
certain to take the line of bewailing the present
conditions and those of the immediate future.
The mechanical reproduction of music is looked
upon with a suspicion that sometimes amounts to
positive terror.   Some comfort themselves with
the assurance that this new endowment of ways
and means can be employed for proselytizing

purposes and for a wide distribution of the commodity which is known as ' a love of good music '. But the fear which underlies all these eager activities can always be felt, and, sometimes, when the conditions are favourable and the doors are fast closed, it is confessed with hysterical vehemence.

That fear is based on a misunderstanding. The mechanical reproduction of music is not only inevitable, but it is also consequential. The simplest kind of music is that for an unaccompanied voice ; for this is the music that is nearest to the original impulse to make music. Experience can be expressed immediately by the voice of him that crieth in the wilderness from his own heart. As soon as other voices join the single voice, even in unison, the experience and the expression are separate, and, with the addition of vocal parts, instrumental music is already foreshadowed. When, therefore, the singer is his own composer, and the composer his own singer, music, ignorant as it may be of its full potentiality, is, nevertheless, at its most blissful stage. How far we are now removed from that stage can be realized when we note how few present-day singers write their own songs and that no composers sing.

The introduction of the first instrument that could produce tone as well as rhythm coincides with the introduction of the first problems of technique, and therefore with the first step

towards sophistication. At once the link with
the original conception is broken, and the question
of interpretation arises. The player must concentrate first upon the taming of his instrument, and
afterwards upon the nature of the music he is to
play. Where the instrument and the music
cannot be reconciled, naturally the instrument
must prevail at the expense of the music, and we
reach the next stage where the player demands
from the composer music which shall be *suitable*
for his instrument. Such music is conditioned
not so much by impulsive experience (although,
conceivably, this may play a small part) as by
physiological considerations. The next stages are
reached through a number of experiments in
combining instruments of various kinds and
qualities. Finally we come to the embarrassing
wealth of a modern orchestra, which calls for a
wise and just chancellor for its proper administration. The importance which the conductor has
lately assumed is entirely due to the fact that
there can be no absolute criterion where performance and conception are separated by a gulf as
wide as that between an unaccompanied folk-song
and (say) Schönberg's *Gurrelieder*. Even the
composer himself sometimes finds it difficult to
recall the precise nature of the experience which
impelled him to write a given orchestral work,
for between that experience and its significant
form lie so many various problems of technique
that it is often more difficult to travel back from

the form to the experience than it originally was to travel from the experience to the form.

And now we have set forth to journey to another stage. For, however much we may stress the word ' mechanical ' in speaking of reproduced or relayed music, it is not very difficult to see that piano-players, gramophones and the wireless represent merely a development of the instrumental phase of music. The shawm and the viol are instruments under the immediate control of the player. The keyed instruments are less directly controlled. The orchestra is a still more complex instrument. And the gramophone and wireless make complexity even more complicated. In this sense we may call the gramophone an instrument. The loud-speaker and the piano-player are instruments. To argue that they are not so because a spring must be wound, or a lever must be pressed, or a battery must be charged, is like arguing that an oboe is not an instrument because the lungs must be charged, and a reed must be shaken by the wind before it will function ; and to argue that they are not so because in their case human agency is twice removed, is merely an unprofitable denial of the benefits of scientific invention, as who should refuse to take a bath because the water is not directly conveyed from the clouds.

Mechanized music is not a retrogression but a logical development, a development which may

7

be called ' intensive instrumentation '.   And since
each successive step in the expansion of musical
means has involved new technical problems, we
are right in expecting this latest phase to present
numerous and peculiar difficulties in connexion
with performance.   At the moment the problems
are almost entirely bound up with the faithful
presentation of reality.   The ideal of all repro-
ducing concerns is to create the illusion that
Pachmann is actually playing to the Digweed
family in their home at Upper Norwood.   But it
is more than likely that this ideal will soon be
renounced or at least qualified.   For it seems
reasonable to suppose that, since instruments
never fail to impose their own conditions upon
the music they are called upon to play, the
engineers of reproduced music, having discovered
their own level, will issue a list of laws and regula-
tions ; and it is equally reasonable to suppose that
composers will take note of those laws, and that
music will be composed specially for the piano-
player or for gramophone reproduction, or for the
purposes of broadcasting.   And in those days it
will not appear irreverent to rearrange the scores
of the older composers who still remain in vogue,
in order to accommodate the peculiarities of the
medium to be employed.

Under these conditions it will be necessary to
revise the existing theories of art.   Hitherto we
have regarded technique as being the outcome,
and, in part, the expression of the artist's

experience ; and whenever this process has been interrupted by the claims of an intractable instrument, we have been justified in qualifying our judgement of the resulting composition. It has now come to pass that the instrument, and not the composition, is all-important. For the time being, we are much more concerned with how the *Choral Symphony* ' comes through ' than with how it comes off as a work ; and seeing that the problems are certain to become more and more subdivided and more and more absorbing, it is certain that conception will gradually become the result and not the cause of technique.

Then we shall be further than ever from the simple melody sung by the lonely of heart.

5

Already there are signs that the relationship of conception and technique is being reversed. The exploitation of atonality by certain composers and of the quarter-tone scale by others does not imply, as they and their advocates naïvely attempt to persuade us, that they have met with a vision on the way and heard a voice saying : ' Renounce and denounce the old order ; for in it there is no life and no hope of inspiration. Henceforth you will be endowed with the faculty of overhearing music which is without tonality, and in which the semitone is halved again. Write down this music, for it is your new inheritance.' Unhappily, the procedure is less mystical than this. The revolution which has been effected in certain quarters is as coldly theoretical as it is relentless. Tonality has been deprived of its kingship, and a mere negative has been set up in its place. The Tone has been hung and quartered. Tyranny flourishes.

Clearly, no music which is governed by these systems can have been conceived according to the laws of nature. For no music that is worth the name has been born in a ready-made suit. The technique of a Mozart opera, or a Beethoven sonata, or a Schubert song is the result of a long series of exact measurements, practised workmanship, and careful fittings. In theory this clothing may be of less account than the inspiration which is to be clothed, but in practice we find that the life and movement of the inspiration depend upon the texture and cut of its garments. What has happened in the case of the atonal and quarter-tone composers ? They have concentrated upon a new style of garment before the conception has been brought to life. They have taken pains to count their unhatched masterpieces. They are expecting, merely.

This is not to say that they will be disappointed. Indeed it is more than likely that, through their constant and concentrated application, works

will be forthcoming that will demand not only a
hearing, but will create the demand for a further
hearing, and finally a few will become established
as classics of the new era. At first we shall
expect to find atonality (and the rest of the
systems) flirting and even effecting a compromise
with the harmonic music of later romanticism.
And, after the house has been set in order, we shall
further expect the arrival of composers, who have
so far absorbed the new principles that they will
be able to set their fancy free. At any moment
during that era there may arise that genius, in
whom all the consciousness of the preceding years
will culminate, and who will at last restore the
rightful order of experience and expression. It
is possible, of course, that such a man will be
recognized and acclaimed by those of his own
generation, more especially since the critical
faculty of the musical public will have been kept
in continual practice by the swift uses of advertisement. But there is no safety in such an
assumption ; for the very efficiency of publicity
methods may defeat this end by insisting upon
the increased birth-rate of heaven-sent composers.
This, however, is of little account beside the fact
that the arrival of the genius is inevitable. For
history teaches us that music is a movement, and
one that does not so much depend upon human
agency as upon its own natural laws. Men are
drawn irresistibly into the movement ; the
power of music enlists them to carry out its

laws. That is why the really great composers could never be justly accused of being charlatans. They wrote in spite of themselves, and some of them shortened their lives by their devotion to the cause. The movement goes on as before, and more composers are enlisted than ever. We complain that too many people write music nowadays ; that they have no sense of direction ; that they are only making confusion worse confounded. The complaint has no real basis. In spite of the feverish activity of contemporary composers, the direction is very clear.

It is certain, for example, that we are nearing the end of the phase which can be called Profuse Harmony. That tree has been cultivated to grow so extensively and to throw out so much foliage, that every conceivable instrument of the orchestra has been able to lodge under the shadow thereof. The time has come for the tree to be pruned, and with the thinning process, many of the instruments will find themselves out in the cold. That is to say, music will become more simple in its process and incidentally more vocal. Howbeit, the new simplicity will not be like the old ; it will not discard all former experience, but imply that experience with a more direct force. A single sound, so to speak, will signify not only itself but also the adventures that have brought about its final resolution. Music will be more simply expressed, but musical experience will be more

complex than ever before. And since the voice
is the most direct and transparent medium for
musical expression, it seems that composers of the
immediate future will concentrate more and more
upon vocal forms. Some will seek to expand the
older forms ; others will require singers to
extend their technique in order to accommodate
a less obvious kind of expression.

Above all, it is likely that choral music will be
reformed. The tendency of late has been to
write for voices as if they were instruments.
This is not so surprising when we realize that the
phase of musical history from which we are now
emerging has been mainly an instrumental phase.
The expeditions which have been carried out
in the harmonic territory have naturally led to
endless permutations and combinations of instruments, since harmony and instrumental colour
are almost identical terms. And whenever a
composer of this period has been moved to write
a choral work, almost invariably he thinks of his
chorus as an orchestra. He requires the basses
to hum, the sopranos to put their hands over
their mouths, the tenors to clench their teeth,
the contraltos to whistle like the wind, and so on—
he wants everything, in fact, but outright singing. This craze for colour-effects is the result of
a complete misunderstanding of the function of
choral music, which is to effect a synthesis of
interdependent voices.

Most of the important choral works of the last

twenty-five years have insisted upon the conflict
and divergence of the voice-parts. Hearing
them, it is impossible to recognize any clear
outline. If history does not repeat itself in the
literal sense of the term, it can certainly indicate
future tendencies; and one of the indications
is that choral music is about to assert its
individuality and revolt against the impositions
of an instrumental style. Vocal parts will run
more fluently, and, running, will assert their close
relationship. Polyphonic music, with a fuller,
riper experience, will come again into its own.

6

Before polyphony comes into its own once
more, it will be necessary to discover and banish
the pretentious thing that now passes for polyphony. For most of the so-called contrapuntal
writing which is practised by contemporary
composers is a sham. It is mere paper currency
with no real value whatever. A young composer,
showing you the score of his new symphony—
' which is going to be played at the next International Festival, you know '—will be careful to
point out to you the subtle points of imitation,
the crafty little canonic devices, the fugal capacity
of his theme. These things will appear plainly
enough in the manuscript, but, when you listen

to an actual performance of the work, devil a canon or point of imitation will you apprehend, for all that you are forewarned. For the fact is that polyphony is utterly misunderstood by the majority of present-day composers. The snippets which serve for their thematic material are visualized rather than auralized, and so long as they make their appearance at the various junctures of the score, it matters not whether these appearances are audibly significant, so to speak. Composers forget that the letter of polyphonic law proceeded from the spirit, and the devices are the merest accidents of musical experience. For the essence of polyphony is the just relationship of the parts, and from this the music gathers momentum. That relationship need not be fixed by any ' table of kindred ', but it must be a *relationship* ; that is to say, the parts must have some common denominator which the ear can detect without the assistance of the score. And, on the whole, it will be found that the surest way of establishing that relationship is to give the parts a vocal quality ; even if they are to be played by instruments, they should be voice-parts. The genius of Bach is found in his application of the principles of polyphonic writing to instruments and to voices used instrumentally. But in doing so he did not—and, indeed, could not— sever connexion with the past. His conceptions were coloured by the vocal music of the centuries before him. The human voice cannot be denied ;

or, if ever it is denied, it will assert its rights with redoubled strength.   Even the last string quartets of Beethoven are not entirely free from vocal colour, and no interpretation of these can satisfy if the parts do not *sing*.

It is the peculiar heresy of the present time that musical tone is conceived with no reference to the voice.   The better half of its endowment has been squandered in crazy speculation.   We have overlooked the point, that if music was made for man, man also makes music for himself, and is for ever being recreated by his own imagination. Music is man's most abstract form of expression ; and the most intimate and direct medium for that expression is his voice.   This simple fact has been obscured by a number of preoccupations.   Chief among them is that which we have already considered under the description of ' mechanized music '.   This intensive instrumentation has had the effect of turning attention away from simple means to complex processes.   We are all so terribly keen to obtain the perfect reproduction, that we pay little or no attention to the perfect reality.   What music can be more real than that of the voice ?   What perfection is more perfect than that of spotless singing ?

Howbeit, there are signs, as I have divined, that the vocal conception of music will be restored.   I have already expressed the opinion that there is no need to be alarmed at the mechanical exploitation of music.   It is evident

that these engineering complexities are emphasiz-
ing a need. That need can be expressed in
the phrase ' tangible personality '. The evolving
technique of broadcasting is chiefly concerned
with how to get personality ' across '. The cata-
logues of the gramophone companies are more
than half filled with vocal records, and the voice
is invading even the secular precincts of dance-
music. The only possible way to keep the larger
public interested in mediate music is to insist
first upon the overwhelming proportions of the
problems to be faced, and, second, upon the
successful solution of those problems. If the
solution is not as successful as at first seemed
likely or possible, there is no reason why the
buying public should know of the shortcom-
ing; for by judicious and intermittent use of
such captions as ' Life-like ', ' Perfection at last ',
' Invite Heifetz to your own home ', etc., amplified
by the faint echoes of weary reviewers, the public
will always believe that the miracle has already
taken place, for the simple reason that belief is
the only efficacious cure for strong desire. The
public would like nothing better than to invite
Heifetz and make him at home; very well then,
supply this need, even with a temporary counterfeit, and the demand will increase. That is
business, and good business too.

The counterfeit, however, is not due to deliberate deception, but to the seemingly tardy
progress of the scientific methods which are

involved. We are not justified in assuming that
the idea of perfect reproduction has been aban-
doned by the engineers. The pianola companies
have made use of analytical notes and even
films to eke out their roll-call. The idea of
synchronizing a vocal performance with a
moving picture of the singer has been successfully
realized.

The feverish experiments which are being
carried out in connexion with television, reveal
with what urgency this phenomenon is desired
for co-operation with broadcasting. The quest
for ' tangible personality ' is a universal obsession ;
so much so that its ultimate discovery in some
form or other can be assumed with reasonable
security. Certainly this assumption is more
defensible than its denial. The argument that
the improbable will never happen because of its
seeming impossibility is being refuted by some
new marvel every day ; and when we confess
that the attainment of ' tangible personality '
seems remote, the reason may very well be that
it is so near at hand that we are unable to recognize its features. The last defence of the argument in favour of its attainment will be found in
the saving clause ' in some form or other '. To
some this may suggest hedging. But is it not
true that all performance is based upon a compromise of this kind ? That is to say, the
playing of *Macbeth* or of a symphony is never any
more than the presentation of the author's idea

in some form or other.   We may go further and
assert that even the author's performance is no
more than the expression of his original conception in some form or other.   So that the
mechanical reproduction of Galli-Curci's voice,
of Sir Oliver Lodge's personality, of Chaliapin's
histrionics, of Pachmann's touch, so long as it
is not an utter distortion, cannot be justifiably
condemned on the ground that it is not actually
and immediately the original.   So long as it
conveys the original with a minimum of impediment, so long as the personality is made sufficiently articulate, we need put no more onus
upon the phrase ' mechanical reproduction ' with
reference to the gramophone than we do upon
the phrase ' voice-production ' with reference
to singing.   The truth is that we have not
yet become so accustomed to the wonders of
mechanical reproduction that we can attend to
the product as a single experience.   We are
preoccupied with unessentials, with incidents
which are the business of the engineers.   As soon
as the engineers bring us to a point where we
can conveniently ignore these incidents, we shall
be in a position to take in the experience as a
whole, just as we do (in theory) in attending to an
actual performance in the concert hall.   And the
influence which will help us most to reintegrate
the experience received from reproduced or
relayed music is that of the voice.   This is another
reason in support of the surmise that we are

entering upon a phase in which the vocal conception of tone will be predominant.

7

At this point, there may be some who are
inclined to turn and answer : 'This is indeed
cold comfort. We are given to understand that
the virtuoso will ultimately be crushed by
mechanized music ; and yet we are bidden not
to be alarmed by the growing power of this
phenomenon—to count the sundry blessings
which it will bring in its train.' The reply to this
objection is that the invasion of mechanized
music is inevitable and that it were better to take
full advantage of the advancing tide than to
drown ignominiously. Doubtless the virtuoso as
we have hitherto known him will be defeated.
He will have had his two centuries or so and will
cease to be of any consequence. But it is equally
certain that, in his stead, a new type of virtuoso
will be evolved, a type that will be adapted to
the new conditions. For already it has become
manifest that the conditions of performance in
a broadcasting or gramophone studio are widely
different from those of a concert-hall performance.
Not only is the absence of an audience a very
important factor in the case, but the technique
itself must of necessity be reorganized. There

are numerous examples of performers who have achieved very highly as recorders or broadcasters and yet have lamentably failed whenever they have been faced with an audience ; and there are examples of opera singers who are impotent before a microphone. The technique of the studio singer or player must be based upon intimacy. He must visualize, not a standardized audience, but a capricious individual, and then must discover the best way of communicating himself to that individual. If anything, his technique must be a finer development than that of the concert-performer, in the first place because his individualized audience will be able to bring microscopic attention to bear upon his performance, and will be untouched by the subtle influence of crowd-psychology ; in the second place because the impetus of his performance must be derived entirely from his own enthusiasm for the work in hand ; and in the third place because between him and his audience a great gulf is fixed, and his immediate concern must be to bridge that gulf and make it possible to pass over it without peril.

A new virtuosity must therefore be evolved, and one that to a large extent will make the older kind unnecessary. One need not be accused of being too recklessly prophetic if one ventures to assert that within the next decade or so, musical critics will be relieved of the greater part of their burden so far as concert attendance is concerned. That is to say, the pernicious habit of recital-giving will have been broken. Singers and players will no longer be willing to pay a night's rental of a concert hall merely to be able to career through the country with a sheaf of mutilated press-cuttings. The game will not be worth the candle, especially since concert engagements, whether in London or in the provinces, will certainly decrease in number.

It is conceivable that orchestral societies, by following the example of the banking world, may prolong their life by a process of amalgamation ; but the process implies fewer engagements for soloists. Moreover, we cannot expect Fleet Street to remain blind to the changing conditions. Editors have always been reluctant to admit music to the sanctuary of their columns, and those who have done so, naturally look for a substantial return in the way of advertisements. As soon as there is the slightest sign of a falling-off in the advertisements, it is certain that there will be a corresponding decrease in the space allotted to music-making. The problems of newspaper make-up are never wholly solved. They recur daily. The word ' space ' is engraved upon the heart of every editor. He must not only be assured that each square inch is profitably occupied, but that it is read by a sufficiently large or powerful section of his public. Whenever he detects (and there are sure ways of doing so) that

a given feature is becoming less interesting to
his readers, he either reforms the feature or
drops it altogether. The latter course is the
more common. No newspaper, however prosperous, can afford to carry a passenger in the
boat.

How many people read the criticisms of
recitals ? They are probably confined to those
immediately interested in the recitalist, those who
' follow ' a given critic, either out of pathetic
idolatry or to entangle him in his speech, and a
handful of people who are engaged upon some
curious statistical project, such as a diary of
musical wisdom or recording the number of times
the *Leonora No. 3* was performed between Septem-
ber 1st, 1928, and March 1st, 1929. These groups
together form a very small percentage of the
musical public, and it is very clear that the
future conditions of performance will not favour
an increase, but rather a considerable decrease
in the numbers. As surely as atmospheric
pressure is registered by a barometer, this
decrease will be registered in the editorial offices.
Space will then be readjusted, and concert notices
will be rejected as superfluous matter. In these
circumstances, the critic will rarely need to travel
in order to find the pretext for his labours.
Without moving from the privacy of his own
study from one year's end to another, he
will yet be able to keep abreast with the
activities of the musical world. Nothing of

8

importance need escape him. Moreover, since
he will no longer be enjoined to supply criticism
straight from the mint of his immediate experience
—since there will be no further need for him to
form a definite opinion of a work at first hearing
and within five minutes of his having received
merely a physical impression thereof—there is
every reason to suppose that music criticism will
be of a less ephemeral order than it is at present.
We may expect to read critical writings which
have been completely purified of journalistic
dross, and which are the result of a more scientific procedure. Under the present order, the
critic rarely has the opportunity of viewing anything but a succession of trees. Only the most
exceptional intuition and the keenest perception
enable him to see the wood as a whole or even to
discover a path that will lead him out of it. The
more private kind of routine implied by the
coming conditions of music-making will probably
reduce his daily allowance of leisure, but since
he will be less closely pressed by editorial commands, and required to send in a less particular
account of recent happenings, he will have greater
opportunity for standing aside and regarding
contemporary music as a general movement.
At such a time music criticism will enter into the
inheritance which awaits it, and be more worthy
of the art it seeks to expound. It will be less
voluble, yet more articulate ; less provincial, yet
more alert ; less arbitrary, yet more inexorable.

As Monsignor Perrelli would have said, it will couple 'glacial judgement with fervent sympathy'.

8

Let me forestall the more controversial type of reader, who has probably remarked that this forecast has left out of account one important field of musical activity. Opera has not been so much as mentioned. The very sound of the word suggests insurmountable difficulties.

To begin to discuss opera, it is necessary to clear the mind of all preconception. It is even necessary to ignore most of the evidence which has been collected, since this evidence is not only conflicting and confusing, but, for the most part, passionately prejudicial. Few people are constitutionally able to take part in any examination of the subject without being shaken by almost primitive emotions. Those who hold that opera as a form of art is unutterably absurd, usually concentrate their attack upon the Wagnerian tradition, and completely ignore the fact that opera is essentially an Italian export ; and if perchance they remember to make Italian opera the object of their venom, they almost invariably base their arguments upon the paucity of good texts and the crippling banality of the bad texts. As if good literature were essential to good opera! As if, indeed, good literature were not sometimes an impediment! Opera is merely an excuse for three hours' continuous singing. There is no other way of maintaining public interest in the vocal art for so long a period. The events which are related matter not at all, so long as they are feasible and can be easily comprehended. The text is only a pretext. I have often wondered why Ernst Krenek has not called upon Gertrude Stein for a libretto. Together they could evolve an opera which would be sure of publicity from the start. The success of *Jonny spielt auf* would be overshadowed by an opera with the title *Spielt Jonny auf Hebee-Jebee auf Spielt Jonny Jebee.*

On second thoughts, no. The persistent accentuation of Miss Stein's inventions would be a burden too heavy for any lyrical phrase to bear. Three hours of song to such unrelieved irregularity would drive us from the opera house for ever; there is even the risk that any one of us, hearing it, might be driven insane, under the impression that he was a metronome out of repair. The libretto of an opera must avoid not only superior distinction as literature, but also any suspicion of eccentricity and freakishness; so that from either point of view Gertrude Stein must be ruled out of court, with my apologies for causing her appearance in the argument to be so brief.

This insistence upon a text with a literary

flavour is at the root of the trouble we have had
and still are having with English opera. You
will never find any nation which is opera-loving
by nature indulging in theories and discussions
about the art of opera. It knows and has always
known so well what opera is and should be, that
it has no inclination to argue over its constituent
parts. It takes those parts, and especially the
libretto, for granted.

The Italian opera composers, of course, were
not careless in their choice of subject and text,
but they were not so much concerned with the
literary value of the text as with the opportunities it provided for the lyrical moment. In
England we are far too much preoccupied with
meticulous and detailed criticism to be a great
opera nation. We are too fastidious to catch the
nearest way. There is no country in the world
where so many articles are written upon the
question of opera, where it is the subject of so
many debates, conferences, and inquiries as in
England ; and this does not necessarily argue
that as a nation we desire opera intensely, but
can find no pioneer to establish it for us ; that
we long for our national form of opera but can
find no composer who will coincide with that
form. On the contrary, we have the pioneers
and we have the composers. This feverish and
self-conscious activity reveals no unanimous
aspiration towards an opera regime ; it merely
discloses the lamentable truth that the opera-lovers

in this country, for all their courage, zeal and enterprise, form an exceedingly small minority. Why, then, should they not acknowledge that they are but a tiny section of the population and establish themselves as a community seeking and obtaining their own desires? Why should they attempt to proselytize? The answer is plain: this particular section of the community, like a few others, but unlike most, cannot realize their ideals without the financial support of some of the other more indifferent sections.

For opera is a fabulously expensive luxury. It is too great a responsibility, too much of a gamble, to attract even the most whimsical of our plutocrats for long. Do you think that this minority of opera-lovers would be so anxious to convert the others if they could raise the money among themselves? I do not deny their enthusiasm and spirit, but it is hardly necessary to assign to them such an altruistic idealism as this. Wherever opera is an established institution, it is so because it is founded upon tradition and patronage. There can be no future for opera in England if we cannot find some organization which will play for us the same rôle that the local courts used to play in Germany.

There are some people who hold that the more important question is: Has opera, as a form of art, any future at all? But, surely, the future of the art-form depends upon the successful administration of operatic enterprise ? Others again will dispute the assertion that in order to flourish, opera must have tradition and patronage as its foundations, and they point to America to bear out their contention. But what do we find there ? When we speak of opera in America we are referring chiefly to organizations such as the New York Metropolitan, the Philadelphia Civic Opera, the Philadelphia Grand Opera and the Chicago Civic Opera, for these are the places where operatic activities are for the most part centred. Moreover, it is erroneous to think of opera in America as a democratic movement. If we take numerical support as the standard, opera is far behind the other forms of musical activity. Whereas symphony concerts, recitals, music clubs, and musical organizations in schools are flourishing all over the country, the average American is still untouched by opera ; and when it comes to the question of the operatic stage as a career for American student-singers, it is an acknowledged fact that comparatively few of them have any chance of success, seeing that they must compete with singers of the highest rank from the Vienna Staatsoper, the Berlin Staatsoper, from Milan, Madrid, Moscow and Paris.

In theory, there should be no difference between the positions of opera in America and in England. It is not higher culture, but greater wealth, applied with greater intelligence and generosity by her rich men, that enables America to run opera in various centres. Of course, the money question makes all the difference to the facts ; but the principle remains the same. America is an eloquent example of the fact, that in order to make opera successful, you must create a habit of mind ; and a general habit of mind cannot be created in a single generation. In those places where opera is a habit among Americans, it is so because wealthy people have had the courage and the imagination to support something which appeared to be desirable. In England we have not only lacked the wealth to establish opera, but also the courage and the imagination.

9

Can we create an opera habit of mind in England ? Here, it may be profitable to find what has made opera a habit of mind in a country where it is run successfully. In Germany, for example, opera is an established thing, a fixed factor. It can point to an honourable history. It is not a sudden craze, due to the enterprise of a promoter with an eye for business, but an institution due to an aristocracy with an eye for culture. It is the effect of the beneficent influence of Court life, exercised in a number of centres throughout the land ; and the vitality of the culture has been encouraged by the inevitable rivalry which sprang up between one centre and another.

In this country, we have no such safe foundation for the establishment of opera.   Our popular institutions—the Music Hall, Association and Rugby Football, etc.—are democratic in nature and origin, and practically all our capacity for competition is expended upon these.*   Sport is an institution with us primarily because it appeals to our insatiable desire for enacted conflict ; and the music-hall turn that can make some reference, either verbally or by a parade of colours, to a well-favoured football team is certain of success.

The average Englishman loves to witness a well-staged match of skill ; but this instinct is founded upon no thwarted passion for revenge, no sneaking, perverted lust to kill.   There must be no obvious danger to life in the Englishman's games.   The bull-fight could make no appeal therefore.   The pursuit is too violent, its implication too deadly.   On the other hand, any game that maintains an even tenor of reasonable rivalry, and at the same time provides a series of incidents not too subtle or technical for the appreciation of the layman, is an irresistible attraction to the English public ; and from this

*It may be noted incidentally, that the rapid growth of the competition festival movement in this country is closely connected with a wise encouragement of local rivalry.

fact, we are entitled to infer that a similar psychological attitude is assumed by the Englishman
in the theatre. If his interest is to be main-
tained, he must be aware of some kind of conflict—either the kind that interests him with a
make-believe tragedy, or the kind that will cause
the convulsion of laughter. Now, the libretto of
the average opera provides him with no spur
to prick on his intent. Many of the stories are
full of the conflict of tragedy, of course, but they
are usually presented in such a preposterous
fashion that the Englishman's sense of fitness
is shocked ; and even those that are not quite
so naïve or outrageously comic become staled
by the persistent performances, which are given
because of the sad illusion that these works are
' old favourites '. ' But you are altogether ignoring the most important factor in the presentation
of opera,' is an objection I seem to overhear.
' Even assuming that the tawdry enactments of
opera appeal no longer to the average Englishman, surely he will be aware of the significance
of the music ; surely this will satisfy his ex-
pectancy of conflict ? '

This ' surely ' is the sign of a Utopian mind.
In an ideal state of things the answer would be,
' Yes, most surely ' ; but in this actual instance
the answer is ' Certainly not ' ; and it is precisely
because the average Englishman is so insensible
to the full import of the music of an opera, that
he misses the whole point of opera as a form of

art. It is useless to analyse for him the functions of music in opera, to explain that the music was conceived as an intensification of the stage-action, as an index to the characters in the drama and their relationship, and in order to create the environment of the play—the ' atmosphere ' as we call it ; for this analysis calls for a corresponding analytical state of mind in the theatre, and the Englishman dislikes being given anything in the nature of a problem when he has set his mind upon enjoyment. This attitude could be more clearly observed, if it were possible to make some kind of statistical inquiry in connexion with the popularity of the various English games as spectacles. But even without the statistics it is evident that horse-races, Association and Rugby Football and boxing, wherein the object is plain, the action, swift, and the procedure, simple, attract by far the largest crowds ; and any game, in which the action is retarded and in which appreciation of the players' *finesse* necessitates a more intimate knowledge of the technique (cricket, for example), is proportionately less popular. The case of opera in England roughly corresponds with that of these more intricate games. The popular works of opera répertoire are so because, as with a prize-fight, the issue is clear.* That is to say, the larger public attends these operas knowing full well the reason for its attendance. It has come

* I am not referring to the result of the fight, of course !

to enjoy certain moments, which for a variety of
complex reasons produce a thrill. In a prize-
fight this thrill is produced by the knock-out
blow ; and the tenor in *Rigoletto* knows that he
can produce a similar thrill by carefully administering the most resonant of his high notes.
Indeed, I recall an incident which proves the
literal truth of this. It occurred during a pre-
war performance at Covent Garden. My neigh-
bour in the gallery was a pleasant, unshaved,
unwashed fellow in cap and scarf. He chewed
gum and was garrulous. After *La donna è mobile*,
however, he suddenly became reserved ; instead
of joining in with the frenzied applause, he turned
to me to make one simple remark : ' That's a
knock-out ! '

For those works where the momentary thrill
is supplanted by a more dispersed and continuous appeal, where the intellect is called into
play ever so slightly, there is no assured support
in this country. It is impossible to imagine a
great success for Boito's *Nerone* here, for example,
since the composer has deliberately curbed his
natural lyrical inspiration ; and as for a work
like Busoni's *Doktor Faust*, in which the appeal
is almost entirely intellectual, it may well be
doubted whether it will ever be produced in
England. And, as I have already remarked,
whenever our own contemporary composers turn
to opera, they are far too self-conscious, far too
intent upon good taste at any price, to produce

a popular masterpiece. Rutland Boughton's
Immortal Hour was the nearest approach to the
solution of the problem ; but his later production,
Alkestis, was so far even from an understanding
of the problem that the earlier success must be
accounted fortuitous.

As for comic opera, for which, we are per-
sistently told, the English have a special aptitude,
there seems to be no real reason to believe that
the Gilbert and Sullivan tradition will be continued by composers. Whenever we wish to
emphasize our national talent for this form, we
are always compelled to fall back upon revivals.
Few living composers are willing to confirm our
faith by producing new examples. They realize
too well, that in the face of American competition
they would stand but little chance of success ;
for the English comic opera tradition has been
completely undermined by the invasion of the
film and the revue.

The genius for opera is the genius for sublimating the ridiculous ; and (in addition to the
reasons already forwarded) it is because the
English are so continually aware of the ridiculous,
that they can so rarely reach the sublime in the
opera house. Howbeit, in spite of these reasons,
we may expect the zealous few to continue their
efforts to establish opera in this country, and
doubtless they will bring forth something that
will appear to be established opera ; but the
simple fact remains that nothing can be

established as a national institution which does not spring from that delicate, irregular organ, the Heart of the Great Public. There is no deeply-rooted desire for opera in England; there is therefore, no overwhelming demand for it, and little hope for those who, out of the fulness of their hearts, come to supply it. In those countries where opera is a matter of fact, it is probable that the tradition will continue automatically. But it is clear that contemporary composers are finding opera an intractable medium for expression. Stravinsky, Krenek, Berg, Goossens, Malipiero, Pizzetti—all these, and many others, have worked through this medium, but it is significant that not one of them has approached the task without some preconceived theory. One abolishes all semblance of a plot; another forswears tonality; another is opposed to lyricism; another restricts the gestures of the singers, and yet another insists that the singers shall be altogether hidden. All these experiments point to a general dissatisfaction with opera as an art-form; so that, although the existing répertoire of operas will continue to be produced so long as the administration of opera is run on sound business lines, it is conceivable that living composers will eventually concentrate upon what they consider to be less dubious forms of expression. We may expect some to evolve from opera a transfigured form which will approximate to a blend of pageantry and ballet; but the more universal tendency is to rescue the art of music from all the encumbrances of romanticism, to purge it of all extraneous significance, and to establish its self-sufficiency.

TALKING ABOUT MUSIC

THERE has never been a time when music was more widely ' appreciated ' than it is now. It is necessary, however, to qualify the word ' appreciation ' with inverted commas. People are too prone to assume that because music is being discussed, reproduced, relayed and noised abroad in a hundred different forms and fashions, the community at large is entitled to claim that elusive virtue which is vaguely described as ' being musical '. The virtue, if such it is, has been not so much achieved as thrust upon us by scientific discovery and by commercial activity. Certainly it is not the result of an overwhelming desire springing from the man in the street. That strange person has been so lethargic in responding to musical stimulus in the past, that his sudden interest at the present time points to some artificial cause. Even so, it would be altogether wrong to ignore this new enthusiasm, and those who have undertaken the task of regulating it, are fully assured that by careful observation they will be able to encourage a natural reaction to music.

These good-natured people, however, are meeting enormous difficulties. They are, to all intents and purposes, physicians. Their task calls not only for knowledge, but also for wisdom and endless patience. The most successful of them, Sir Walford Davies, owes his success to a talent for putting himself, not condescendingly, but instinctively, in the position of the patient. That is one of the surest ways of diagnozing the disease or the complaint ; it also wins the patient's confidence and helps him to rally. The trouble is, of course, that there are so many patients and such a great variety of disaffections. There are those who are organically afflicted, those who are seriously ill, those who are invalids, and those who are merely indisposed. The first and the last of these groups are the most difficult to deal with, for they refuse to co-operate with the physician in his efforts on their behalf—the first type because he is unable, the last type because he is unwilling. The others are never really hopeless cases, for they are always ready to give a more or less accurate account of their symptoms. I consider that these accounts are most important, for they are the only reliable data which the physician receives. Some of the accounts are so violently prejudiced as to be practically useless ; others are so distorted by hypochondria that it is difficult to find the true perspective. But the evidence as a whole provides a very valuable source of information, even when it is most conflicting.

The nature of some of the difficulties which listeners encounter in attending to musical programmes can be indicated by citing one or two examples. Here is a quotation from a letter which I received after one of the talks on ' Next Week's Broadcast Music ' (I have chosen this one as being the most frequent type of letter) : ' . . . I wonder if you can help me to solve a problem which has been troubling me for some time past. I can appreciate Wagner's music almost without exception, Chopin, and most of Schumann. Haydn I find dull for the most part. But I have no conscience about him. I have a conscience, however, about my inability to care for Bach. I feel that the fault is mine. How can I remedy it ? '

The conscience-stricken listener presents a special problem. He is represented in large numbers in every kind of audience, whether in the concert hall, the opera house, or as a listener to the B.B.C. programmes. The stumbling-block is not the same in each case. Very commonly it is Bach (as in the case quoted above), at other times it is Beethoven, or Wagner, or Strauss, or Mozart. The most hopeful sign in these cases is the *desire* to esteem. The physician can at least be sure that he is not up against any active opposition, but his difficulties are none the less on that account. They are greater, rather, since the hidden opposition is probably due to some kind of inhibition. Clearly it cannot be removed, except by individual attention spread over an extended period, a responsibility, of course, which

no broadcaster can undertake. Meanwhile the
most that can be done is to advise warily in
some such reply as this : ' Do not expect from
Bach the things that Bach cannot give. Perhaps
you listen to his music with a mind and a judgement already coloured by Wagner's music. In
any case listen actively, and try, as an experiment, to follow an inner part (the tenors or
contraltos if the work is choral) right through
a given movement. You will at least become
interested in the progression of the music, and
that is a big step in the right direction.'

The listener who cannot ' deal with ' contemporary music is a difficult type to meet,
chiefly because in a number of cases the physician
himself is unable to certify the symptoms and
their proper treatment. Here is a case : ' Following your instructions, I carefully listened to
the Béla Bartók concert. I love every note and
every progression in *Till Eulenspiegel* ; in fact, all
Strauss, including the *Alpine Symphony*, which
I consider a magnificent thing ; but last night's
Béla Bartók concert was, to me, terrible.
Nothing from a melodic, harmonic, or structural
point of view. In addition, an atmosphere of
trivial puerility. What waste of a symphony
orchestra's time ! '

This is really useful evidence, since the writer
first of all gives us an example of what music he
can enjoy, and afterwards gives the reasons for
his dislike of Bartók's works. The difficulty in

this case is to persuade the listener that, contrary to his statement, Bartók's music *has* a structural and harmonic basis, but one altogether different from preconceived ideas of structure and harmony. Here, again, individual attention is necessary if the cure is to be complete, and here again, the broadcaster must resort to temporary measures and assure the listener (if he himself is convinced of this) that the composer is in earnest, that he is anything but a charlatan, and that his fame is established upon authoritative grounds. When all is said, there is no absolute necessity for any listener to accept the music of Bartók, Schönberg, Webern, Hindemith, Honegger, etc., without reservation. Musical salvation is conditioned by the laws of heredity, period and environment.

On one occasion I received from a listener a letter in which she asked, ' Who, in your opinion, is the greatest composer ? ' This was my reply :

' DEAR MADAM,

' I think, perhaps, the correct answer to your question is " I quite agree." That question, " Who is the greatest ? " has been asked ever since the world began, and no satisfactory answer has yet been given. The measurement of human achievement is relative and arbitrary. We can never define greatness ; we can only be aware of it. And in the end we are forced to admit that one great composer differs from another great composer as distinctly and definitely as he differs from a great river or a great athlete. That is, his greatness is his own exclusive property, which gives no ground for comparison with other greatnesses, except in so far as it is great.

'In a recently published volume on Beethoven, the author attempts to establish that Beethoven is a greater composer than Bach, or Mozart or Wagner. I find his method unconvincing. It is the prize-fight method. He brings Beethoven into the ring to stand up against each of the other fellows, and, since the author himself is the referee, it is perfectly easy for him to count the others out in succession. Incidentally, he allows one or two doubtful blows to pass, to his own advantage. Nothing is gained by this " World's Championship " method of criticism. To attempt to prove that Beethoven's *Mass in D* is one of the greatest of all musical works by asserting that the *Kyrie* of Bach's *B Minor Mass* is as aesthetically valuable as " the sight of a company of the Guards marching past the colours with an almost absolute regularity of rhythmic perfection," seems to me to be utterly useless. Surely it is enough to prove that Beethoven's *Mass* is one of the really great works by concentrating upon its intrinsic merits. And this is not a difficult task.   There is no need to drag in Bach, and subject him to what amounts to an insult.

' Forgive me, madam, if I appear dogmatic, but it seems to me that this mania for irrelevant comparison is the chief weakness of contemporary criticism.   Even one of our respected poets has been heard to remark that Shakespeare could put Milton in his hat.   He should have known better.   We may be sure that such a thought would never have occurred to Shakespeare !   But   in this utilitarian age, when everything, from a packet of tea to a symphony, must be weighed and labelled, it is very difficult to resist the impulse to set off one achievement against another, and odiously to compare them.   Do you remember the controversy which was raging some time ago under the heading " Jazz *versus* Straight Music " ?   It is hardly likely that you have forgotten it.   Well, there you had a symptom of the mania.   In the first place, the title of the dispute was an unfortunate invention, for it implied that jazz was in some way " crooked " music.   Nothing could be further from the truth.   Jazz is not only the straightest kind of music, but also the most rigid so far as rhythm is concerned.   Occasionally one meets with a jazz-band which exercises a little imagination, and refuses to insist upon 1–2–3–4 with the aid of field artillery.   On these occasions one encounters very little tonal perversion, no decapitated trumpets, no gagged trombones, no bowler hats. But, as I say, the occasions are very rare, and as a general rule, jazz is as straight as a die ; so that to stage a fight between jazz and so-called straight music is like arranging a match between Tunney and himself.

' But my real quarrel with the question " Which do you prefer, Jazz or Symphony ? " is that it is utterly absurd. What would you answer if I asked you, " Which do you like better, grape-fruit or the dome of St. Paul's Cathedral ? " There is no answer. The one is a question of idle amusement, the other, a question of aesthetic experience.

' And your question " Who is the greatest composer ? " belongs to the same order of absurdity (I hope you will not misunderstand me), for it is based upon this unreasonable and unreasoning craze for lists and orders of merit. It is all due to our peculiar education. When we are at school we are pursued by lists from week to week ; and when we reach man's estate we are still pursued by lists in the form of Football League tables. With so much continual rivalry in the air, it is not surprising when a listener writes (as one wrote to me recently) expressing a desire to promote César Franck from the Second to the First Division, or when many listeners unite to demand the relegation of Béla Bartók for his recent bad form.'

.   .   .   .   .

One of the most frequent questions that I encounter in letters from listeners is 'What is good music ? ' The question is asked in a number of ways, and I always attempt to simplify the matter by putting the question in a new form : ' What is goodness in music ? ' Not long ago I met with the naïve assertion that good art is that which arouses in us emotions stronger than ourselves. But surely this eternal question of good and bad art cannot be dismissed quite so hastily ? Take an ordinary example. Let us assume that a man is disturbed in his sleep by some well-meaning but vocally unfit carol-singers. They are bidding him to do that which he is most loath to do, ' to salute the happy morn ', and the summons contains no quality either of intrigue or glamour. At first, the sufferer attempts to preserve a philosophical calm and comforts himself with the thought that the ill-bred performance will soon be ended. When he finds that his hopes are unfounded, and that the singers have lulled themselves into a kind of perpetual song, he finds that, despite all his efforts, his indignation increases with every moment, until finally his emotions become stronger than himself, and he precipitates himself into some violent action of revenge. According to the definition given above, the stimulus which was responsible for this emotional disturbance must be accounted ' good art ', whereas ordinary opinion, obsessed by no theoretical assumption, merely describes it as an infernal nuisance.

But let me be more generous. Let me assume that the assertion, that good art is that which arouses in us emotions stronger than ourselves, refers to aesthetic experience—the power in us of taking things as they are and appraising them at their proper value, without reference to their context or our own. This isolation of judgement is an extremely difficult process. Indeed, in a world crowded with experience of every kind, it is almost impossible to acquire it ; it must be inherent, and even so it must be constantly and purely employed lest it fall into disrepair. But the existence of this power does not of itself explain the nature of goodness in art. It only shows it to be a relation. We listen to the Beethoven Trio, opus 97 ; we receive a series of impressions ; the series is telescoped into a single impression ; we judge that impression to be something that can be accepted and delighted in without question ; also as something not yet fully exhausted and therefore as something desirable. All those qualities in the experience and all the others that are implied, constitute the goodness therein. But this goodness lies in the experience, not in the thing experienced,

Human nature, however, is perverse and illogical. Whenever anything happens to the average man, he at once transfers the quality of the incident to its immediate cause. It seems a perfectly natural thing to do. If he is stung by a wasp, he looks upon the wasp as a creature with a stinging retort; the wasp, on the other hand, looks upon itself as a creature with a provision for self-protection.

It is important to realize how strong is this habit of transferring qualities from the experience to the cause of the experience. It is the most common of all human errors. Yet it is not so serious an error after all, since it is reasonable to assume, that there must be some intimate relation between the cause and the process of making it effective. (Note that I am not here concerned with cause and effect, only with cause and experience. The first is active, the second is passive.) In some rare cases that relation may become so fine as to appear to have complete identity, but it will only be an appearance. When, however, it comes to defining what 'goodness' in art really is, the most precise thing we can say is this: that quality in any work of art which results in an experience which—according to the definition above—we can call good, is goodness. Yet there are two 'goodnesses', and not merely one, however nearly they may seem to approximate. Some will consider this to be very unsatisfactory as a definition, but, as soon as we attempt to file it down, we find we are discarding some essential condition.

Howbeit, it is possible to classify the idea of goodness a little more rigidly. In applying it to aesthetic experience, I have already specified the qualities of intrigue and self-sufficiency. The experience must hold promise of something as yet unperceived, and it must depend on no external incident or condition for its value. If we give a metaphysical twist to the argument, and conceive an experience as being aware of itself, we may then say that its goodness consists in not only being aware of itself but in being completely satisfied with itself. In that sense we have hit upon the literal meaning of the phrase, ' Goodness only knows '.

In addition to these attributes there is another, which we may call aptitude. We find this significance in the very word itself. *Good* has as its root *godoz* which is a strong version of *gad*, meaning ' fit '.

We need not be afraid that the addition of this meaning will so far widen the sphere of art that artistic creation will lose caste. It is impossible to deny that a saxophone, quite apart from the music it makes (which is another matter), is well-adapted to its end, and therefore is, from the point of view of an instrument-maker, a work of art : the same holds true of the *Mauretania* and a fountain-pen. ' Must we then classify these

things with the *B Minor Mass* and *Tristan* ? ' you
will ask. Yes, all these are in a class together.
' And is their value uniform ? ' No, for we have
an important criterion. Just as the degree of
suitability will determine the class, so the value
(real or apparent) of the purpose that is served
will determine the position in the class. The
Mauretania may be bringing the whole of the
Philadelphia Orchestra over to London in order
to perform the *Eroica* symphony. In such a case
it will be serving a great and noble purpose. But
this purpose is subservient to the purpose of the
symphony itself, and this, among a multitude of
other reasons, gives us the right to judge the
Mauretania in this circumstance as a lesser work
of art than the *Eroica* symphony. The poem,
and the fountain-pen used for its inscribing, may
be similarly placed by using this same system.

It follows, therefore, that in so far as a Charleston-tune succeeds in achieving its end, namely
to incite people to dance the Charleston, it is a
good Charleston-tune. But, as we have seen, it
has other conditions to fulfil before we are justified
in assigning to it the quality of superlative goodness. The tests are : (1) Is it enjoyable in itself,
apart from the violent disturbance of equilibrium
which it produces ? (2) For how long is it
enjoyable ? In answering these questions we
must take various individual experiences into
account, but not so far as to allow them to be a
stumbling-block. For it is also possible to make

a more general observation, and to say that a work of art lives by reason of its inherent health and vigour, and not merely by the artificial respiration supplied by a temporary fashion. A revival of a once-popular play, or opera or symphony merely indicates that a few influential people still believe in the work and wish to communicate their belief to others. If they fail to do this, then *ipso facto* their judgement is proved to be erroneous—always assuming, of course, that the conditions of the revival are favourable. It means that they are attempting to make alive what has long since been dead and cannot live again (e.g. the recent revival of *The Huguenots* at Covent Garden). On the other hand, a work full of glowing life may be allowed to fall into neglect by an indifferent generation. When the time comes for the revival of such a work as this, it invariably responds to the warmth of human affection (e.g. Sir Hamilton Harty's performance of Berlioz' *Requiem* given in the Albert Hall about two years ago). However widely the tastes of individuals may vary, they cannot persist to any serious extent before a work of enduring life and beauty, whose seed is in itself.

THE MAN IN THE STREET

I HAVE a friend, who, from time to time, calls on me ' to do a bit of straight thinking ', as he puts it. On one occasion we were discussing ' appreciation ', and I advanced one or two of the opinions which are expressed in the preceding essay. When I used the phrase ' the man in the street ', my friend remarked : ' I believe there is no such person. But I realize, of course, that there are many people who not only believe in his existence, but are constantly addressing themselves to him. It is significant, however, that the address is almost invariably indirect. There is no immediate contact. The phantom must be approached either through the medium of broadcasting or through books on " appreciation ". The world of musical education labours very heavily under the delusion.'

' And the publishers too ? ' I suggested.

My friend was emphatic : ' Of course. *Plain Man's Guide, First Steps into the Concert Hall, Symphonies Without Tears*—books with such titles as these are being poured out almost every month by publishing firms. I cannot imagine who reads them, or, if they are read, what good they are doing. If the man in the street is still in the street, he certainly does not greet his friend with, " Hullo, Bill, what did yer fink of the Idun Kwortett lorsht nah-it ? "   Nor was ever a street-corner brawl begun through a divergence of view as to the merits of Hugo Wolf as a song-writer. Imagine the dismay and the embarrassment of a Hyde Park crowd on being addressed on the subject of " The Tyranny of Sonata Form ".'

.   .   .   .   .

After he had left, I retired to bed, pondering his words.   Perhaps the idea expressed in the last sentence had fascinated my subconscious self, or perhaps . . .   Well, in any case, I had a dream, and in my dream I found myself in the Park, listening to such a speech as my friend had mockingly suggested.   The whole thing seemed peculiarly vivid, especially as my dreams are usually vague, incoherent, idiomatic and altogether beyond verbal translation.   And, because it was vivid and because it truly happened (lest you should suspect journalistic jugglery here) I will set down the dream in terms of daylight and consciousness.   For clarity's sake, I will avoid wholesale phonetic spelling and confine it to the more obvious words.

A young man with black hair, a sallow complexion and deep-set fanatical eyes, was addressing the crowd.   He wore a scarf and carried his cap in his hand.   I had seen this man in real life addressing a similar meeting on behalf of the miners.   In the dream my mind had played a trick.

His banner no longer carried the slogan, ' A Living Wage for the Miner ', but instead, the strange device, ' Fair Play for Brahms '.   At first I merely saw the wild, undisciplined gesticulations of the speaker without hearing his words.   I pressed forward to the front line and found myself in a hotbed of hecklers.   The speech ran a turbulent course :

' I did not say that Brorms was the lorst of the Romantics.'   (Hecklers : ' Yeshyerdid.')   ' What I said was that he was the lorst cumposer tew understand the meanin' o' the word Romantic.' (Hecklers : ' What, with that beard ! '   ' His music is all beaver.'   ' Yer cawn't expect ter find Romance in a bird's nest.' etc.)   ' 'Ere, wait a minute.   One at a time.   'Oo was it said his music is all beaver ?   What abaht the chune in the lorst movement of the First Siffany, what abaht the Violin Senahters, what abaht the Peganinny Variashuns—aren't they clean-shaven enough for yer ?   You fink you know a mighty lot, but I don't serpose many of y'ave 'eard a note of the Variashuns.'   (Heckler : ' Come off it ! The wife plays 'em once a week, and, wot's more, the 'ole set, bofe books.')   ' Well, then, all I can say is that yer oughter be ashamed o' yerself talkin' all that nonsense abaht some of the most magical music man ever made.'   (Heckler : ' You should just 'ear the wife at it ; yer wouldn't call

it magic. It's more like an 'orrible murder.')
' I'm not torkin' abaht interpretashun ; I'm
torkin' abaht the music itself. And if you know
a more tasty slice o' melody than this you can
'ave it.' Whereupon the speaker whistled clearly
and with faultless intonation the opening theme
of Brahms' Violin Sonata in A major, transposing
it an octave higher. This roused a storm of
cacophonous protests. The only one I could
distinguish came from a woman standing near to
me. With an air of confidence she remarked :
' The old man wasn't above a bit o' poaching, was
'e ? That sounds like Walter's Prize Song ter
me.' The crowd was incensed by this quiet
statement, and one man climbed to the platform,
seized the banner, and rending it in twain cried :
' Fair play for a poacher ? In the words of
Bernard Shaw, " Not . . " ' Unfortunately, at
this moment a constable appeared and pushed
his way through the crowd, repeating that
familiar formula, ' Wot's all this ? Wot's all
this ? ' The speaker attempted an explanation,
but the constable was busy fitting together the
fragments of the banner. Having succeeded,
he examined it carefully, then turned and asked
with great deliberation, ' 'Oo is this Brorms ? '

At this the crowd stood still for an instant, then
with one strident voice yelled, ' Wot ? ' Then
the confusion began again. The woman near
me shouted, ' Dip 'im in the Serpentine '. This
was the signal for a rush for the constable. There

was nothing to be done but to give way to the herd-instinct, and soon I found myself caught up by a rising tide of offended dignity, and running with the crowd to help to carry out this suggestion of total immersion.

.   .   .   .   .

My awakening was precipitous. My dream-enthusiasm had run away with me so far that I had plunged headlong from my bed. It was half an hour before I fully regained my normal state of mind. Having done so, I found my convictions shaken, and my principles undermined, especially those concerning music and the man in the street.

'There is no such person,' I said to myself in a loud, clear voice.

CONTEMPORARY ENGLISH MUSIC

THERE are welcome signs that the Continental attitude towards English music is changing. That attitude for some time past has been ' Can anything good come out of England ? '—a question that always implied the answer, ' No ! ' Some time ago a book was published with the title *The Land Without Music*. The author, Oscar Schmitz, summed up this general attitude in the following passage : ' I have long sought to find what really is the deficiency which ever again you feel to underlie so many English qualities, and which has so petrifying an effect. I have asked myself what is the quality which that people lacks ; can it be kindness, love for one's fellows, piety, humour, the artistic sense ? No, all these qualities exist in England, some even more palpably than with us. And in the end I have found what distinguishes Englishmen from all other cultured races to quite an astonishing degree—a defect admitted by every one, hence no discovery of mine, but the significance of which has never, I fancy, so far been pointed out : the English are the only cultured race without a music of their own (music-hall ditties excepted). I say, " music of their own ", for, perhaps, more foreign music is performed in England than in any other country. That means not only that their ears are less discerning, but that their whole inward life must be poorer.'

This criticism already stands in need of justification, and even when it was written, it was clear that the writer had not considered all the available evidence. For in May, 1925, when the Festival of the International Society for Contemporary Music was held in Prague, Vaughan Williams's *Pastoral Symphony* was performed, and was acclaimed with such genuine warmth that one was justified in discerning a new point of view in the Continental criticism of English music. European critics—who formerly looked askance, when they looked at all, at contemporary English music— were obviously considering whether they should not face us fairly and squarely.

This necessitates a corresponding attitude on the part of English critics—one that should be discriminating and excessively self-critical. For not all our living composers are swans, even if they are persuaded that they are of that lineage by the little groups that support them.

In order to understand the music of representative English composers and to appraise their real position, not only in this country, but also on the continent, it is necessary to give some account of the general conditions of musical development which have brought about their several achievements. Dr. Dyboski, lecturing at Prague University recently, pointed out that post-war changes in the English mentality have been partly brought about through Continental influences. These influences have played their part in the recent history of British music, although not with equal effect all round. The two chief musical influences in Europe during the last twenty years are of course those represented by Schönberg and Stravinsky. In England, while we have been disturbed from time to time by the outer rings of the Stravinsky influence, the Schönberg influence has touched us hardly at all. There are a few isolated individuals in England who profess themselves to be ardent disciples of Schönberg, ready to follow into whatsoever dark place he may lead them ; and possibly the recent visit of Schönberg to England has caused a slight revision of critical values ; but it is already manifest that his ' transvaluation of all values ' is merely a negation of value—a philosophy of nothingness. On the other hand, the Stravinsky seed fell upon more fruitful ground in England. Through the medium of the Diaghilev ballet, the nucleus of an important public was prepared, and it was inevitable that the demand of this public should be met by a corresponding supply of British music. In spite of the fact that Stravinsky at this period began to make public confession, that he had never really been completely in love with the theatre, and that he wished to obtain a divorce in order to be able to devote himself to ' purity in music ', he was, nevertheless, unable to hide the fact that his marriage had produced a number of children, all revealing unmistakable signs of their parentage.   Among these we must count Eugène Goossens, Arthur Bliss, and Lord Berners ; and the table of kindred has now been further extended to include a few first-cousins, of whom William Walton and Constant Lambert are the most prominent.   It would be a mistake, however, to assume that the music of these younger English composers can be wholly accounted for by the Stravinsky influence.   The later works of Arthur Bliss, and especially his *Pastoral*, reveal an increasing assertion of individuality, which, although it was never entirely absent from his earlier works, was often obscured by his very marked deference to Stravinskyan ways and means.   Goossens has made no secret of his intense admiration for Stravinsky.   After the first performance of *Les Noces* in London in 1926, he published the following opinion : ' *Les Noces* is not only the most original work of the last twenty years, but it is probably the most effective.   It is the sanest, happiest, and most consistent work of its author, for it achieves what it sets out to achieve—the complete union of spirit and form.'   After reading this opinion we are not so surprised to find that in his later works (the *Sinfonietta* for orchestra and the *String Sextet*, for example) Goossens has turned neo-classicist, just as Stravinsky and Milhaud have turned. We are right to regard this new classical phase with suspicion. When Darius Milhaud makes the statement that the younger French composers are adding to the old harmonies and expanding the old forms, that they have no intention of doing away with the established order of things, I feel inclined to remind him of the truth that new wine cannot be put into old bottles without disaster. Contemporary composers should take heed lest they deceive themselves with easy words and convenient theories. The creation of a work of music to-day differs altogether from the same process two hundred and fifty years ago. The composer then was not only creator, but pioneer. Not only was he inspired, but he had perforce to discover the best means of conveying his inspiration. The tendency to-day is to reverse the process, to concentrate upon the devising of a new form, or the expansion of an old one, and afterwards to seek for the idea that the form can accommodate. This fawning attitude of being only too willing to revere and employ traditional forms, is only another aspect of the desire to destroy them utterly. When, at the end of the sixteenth century, the development of the polyphonic style of music led to such complexity that it became almost incomprehensible, the reaction in favour of homophonic principles happened in the nature of things. There was no thought of attacking the old order. The time for development had come, and those who were found wise and ready, took part in the movement without a backward thought.

This digression is intended to be no more than a warning, and certainly not an attack on neo-classicism. There is no more healthy sign than this desire to return to the principles of good form, always provided that the return is made unself-consciously. Self-consciousness is the chief weakness of the contemporary composer, and the younger English composers are by no means exempt from the charge. Goossens' activities as a conductor tend to increase the danger for him, and cause him to rely too heavily at times upon his brilliant and facile technique.

Lord Berners is also a good technician. The quality of his technique is a result of his contact with Stravinsky and Casella, and also of his own predilections. Continental criticism as a whole regards him as a typical English composer, chiefly because of his quips and capricious humour. In point of fact, he reflects only one facet of English humour and represents only one small group, which can be roughly said to consist of those who have 'travelled a little' and return to England to ridicule essentially English qualities, merely because they are *different* from the essential qualities of other nationalities. For my part, I consider that Lord Berners is at his best as a composer when he is least satirical, for then he is most fluent and dexterous. The material of Music and the material of Ironic Humour do not readily coincide.

When we remember that the members of this group of English composers were born in the 'eighties or early 'nineties, we can judge them more easily by taking some account of the colour of their environment during impressionable years. With the composers born in the 'seventies, the case is very different. They have been used to bring about a transitional phase between the enlightened conservatism of Victorian and Institutional Music and the brilliant and complete emancipation of Georgian and Cosmopolitan Music. The two outstanding men of this group are Holst (born in 1874) and Vaughan Williams (born in 1872). Neither of these composers can be called brilliant or facile. Their technique has been a long, arduous, and (with Vaughan Williams) sometimes a laborious process. This is as much due to the peculiar problems of expression with which they were brought face to face, as to their personal characteristics. For, from Parry and Stanford to Holst and Vaughan Williams, was a much more difficult step than from Parry and Stanford to Goossens and Bliss. When Holst and Vaughan Williams were young men, they were very much alone so far as questions of expression were concerned. They found nothing ready-made which could be turned to profitable account. And certainly it never occurred to them to resort

to an ' explanation ' in the Milhaud vein. They
were never guilty of saying, ' You see, what we are
really after is to give these dear, old, established
forms a new lease of life ! ' And the reason is
clear. Both Holst and Vaughan Williams are
men of a deeply reflective, if not mystical, mould.
And, being musicians too, they were naturally
impelled to express their reflections and their
moods in terms of music. The form of that
expression is, with them, the result of the content,
and not a preconception. And since these composers were compelled to do their own spade-
work in the matter of technical construction,
it follows that the process of finding the most
apt and singular medium was lengthy and often
tantalizing. The pilgrimage of Vaughan Williams
was not only long but devious ; at one period
he discovered himself at the shrine of Ravel, an
influence which had the effect of pointing his
style and making it more flexible. But the
most important factor in directing the course
of Vaughan Williams's development has been the
folk-song element. As I have pointed out elsewhere, his has never been merely an antiquarian
interest. Nor has he ever been urged by any
insolent desire to ' mock the time with fairest
show ' by presenting these old tunes in modern
dress. His way, and it is very clearly revealed
in the *Pastoral Symphony*, is to live intimately and
quietly with this folk-music, and, perchance, to
catch its overtones from time to time, and with

these to weave a texture of sound which calls back those far-off forgotten days and bring them nearer to the veil. The patience and long-suffering of Vaughan Williams's methods (so contrasted with the feverish contrivances of the younger composers) bear fruit in such a work as the *Pastoral Symphony*, where the sweet earthy breath of the English hills resides almost as a reality.

I remember hearing the work played on one occasion in Worcester Cathedral. In such circumstances, it was possible to catch something of what Roger North meant by the ' cool music of temperate summer evenings '. That ethereal song at the end, floating down from above the arches of the nave, seemed to lead one forth from the cathedral environment to the wide and coloured counties beyond.

Holst has also been considerably influenced by folk-music. He also is a West Countryman, and he also studied for a time with the late Sir Charles Stanford. His achievement has not resulted from worldly or circumstantial advantages. On the contrary, he was met by a succession of difficulties in his early career. At the Royal College of Music, for example, his pianoforte and organ studies were interrupted by neuritis in the hand, and after this he studied the trombone.

Incidentally, this study enabled him to assimilate a practical knowledge of the technical side of orchestral writing, and since his subsequent appointments as organist and music-master at churches and schools brought him into close touch with choral work, he was able to combine the two techniques very effectively in such works as *The Hymn of Jesus*, the *Ode to Death*, and a choral symphony which was written for the Leeds Festival of 1925. For a period he was preoccupied with the setting of Hindu epics, and, although this preoccupation cannot be said to have educed his best music, it was more than mere curiosity or superficial pretext, and this theosophical vein continued even in the new phase which opened with the *Planets* suite. Although the great variety of his music prevents the discovery of any very marked characteristic, yet it is possible to point to the intense sincerity of each work. And when I say that his music is intensely sincere, I mean that it never resorts to any trick of composition, that it is direct (even when it is most complex) in its expression, and that it can never be accused of being ' infirm of purpose '.

Between the two groups of composers I have already discussed, there are others whose birth in the late 'seventies or early 'eighties provides yet another link in the chain. Among them are Arnold Bax, John Ireland, and Frank Bridge. In many ways these composers are more characteristic of the cadence of the Romantic Era than Vaughan Williams and Holst, just as Mahler and Bruckner are the true representatives of this cadence in Central Europe. The English composers are prolonging this cadence with such tenacity and fondness, that they form a very ample and relieving contrast to the new strain in English music. English musicians are by no means tired of the work of these three composers. On the contrary, they are continually being called upon for new symphonic and chamber works for performance at important provincial festivals. An example is the orchestral work by Frank Bridge called *Enter Spring*, which was heard for the first time at the Norfolk and Norwich Festival in 1927. In this there are gathered together all the forces of the immediate past in a defiant and full-throated song. The composer seems to be protesting against the march of Time. ' Let us now see,' I hear him shout, ' whether the Romantic Movement is dead. I think you will agree with me that it is not.' The work is a heroic gesture which would have been more aptly entitled *Exit Summer*.

Arnold Bax prolongs the dying fall of Romanticism with more calm and patience as well as with a more natural conviction. His music proclaims the essentially harmonic character of that phase of music with an almost riotous expenditure. His manner is that curious mingling of reflection and effusion which is expressed in the aesthetic application of the word ' rich '. He is the London-Irishman, who can turn overwhelming emotionalism to splendid account by reason of his extraordinary technical facility and his power to endure.   He is never at a loss for something to express ; his problem is rather, how to apportion the excess of his impulses, to organize them and to direct them into eloquence.   When he is furthest from the solution of that problem, we feel that his expression is becoming either diffuse or abstruse and unnecessarily elongated.   When, however, he lights upon the solution of these intensely individual problems, he persuades us, as few other living British composers can, of the truth of the lines from Yeats' play *The Shadowy Waters* :

> What the world's million lips are thirsting for,
> Must be substantial somewhere.

With John Ireland the Romantic spirit is more directly and more vigorously expressed.   He rarely permits himself the luxury of introspection. He submitted himself to French influence for a time, not because of any unhealthy desire to be infected with Latin impressionism, but merely because of a common-sense desire to enrich the funds of his own expression.   There is no more conscientious composer in Europe.   His early works (including four orchestral works, choral works, a string sextet, two string quartets, and a trio for piano, clarinet, and 'cello) have been withdrawn, because he now considers that they misrepresent his aims and development.   He affords a striking contrast to Bax, for, whereas the music of the latter is conditioned by an ever-expanding revelation of harmony, the music of John Ireland is the outcome of a compressed harmonic expression, however much this may be overlaid with *appoggiaturas* and reinforced overtones.

There remain two other great figures among living English composers, but, although these again were born in the same period, they cannot by any stretch of the imagination be associated, unless it be for purposes of differentiation. Elgar is the official composer of England—the musician we instinctively look to whenever a national event is to be organized. Although there is no such national title in connexion with English music, we associate Elgar with the term ' Composer Laureate ' much more readily than we associate Dr. Bridges with the term ' Poet Laureate '.

Delius, on the other hand, is essentially the unofficial composer, a man who has always sought seclusion not only from public life but from musical influences. He is the most natural, ' uncultivated ' (in the best sense of the word) of all English, and, perhaps, of all European composers. His expression is the reflection of a poetic mind. As opposed to Elgar's, which is dynamic even if it is only moving to the sound of the soldier's tread, Delius's music is static.

There are, in his most typical works, episodes

that almost elude the sense of progression. Time and period are dissolved in the spaciousness of a harmony, which, for all its shimmering details, impresses itself upon the senses as an unvaried quality.

There is no such dissolving with Elgar. His music insists upon the elements of time and period, insists so strongly in his symphonic works that we seem to be for ever on the march. If Delius's expression reveals, as I have said, the mind of a poet, Elgar's reveals the mind of a musician, so single a mind as to be almost insensible, not to poetry, indeed, but to the conditions of poetic thought. His essentially musical manner of thinking is clearly revealed in the *Introduction and Allegro* for string quartet and strings, a work which is no less representative than the Symphonies.

I shall not enter here upon a discussion of the sharp division which exists in English criticism over Elgar. It is occasioned merely by a conflict of generations, a necessary phase in criticism, but often a misleading one. It is more important to employ a summary of all that I have written for the purpose of considering the immediate future of musical composition in England. It is clear in my own mind that our insularity—a natural quality in an island people—is an advantage rather than otherwise at the present time. It has not prevented the Stravinsky invasion, but at least it has successfully resisted the

Schönberg influence. It would be useless to deny the power of Schönberg ; there is no greater power in contemporary music. As I have already hinted, the development of music cannot continue as if Schönberg had never been. But his power has been of Darkness and not of Light, and, whereas the younger German composers—Hindemith is a good example—are using their vitality to shake off the Schönberg fetters, having found out their flaw, the younger English composers can use their force for more progressive purposes. They are impeded by no kind of inhibition, and although there is as yet no genius on the horizon, it is possible that the accumulation of the fluent forces of numerous talents will ultimately swell into the full flood of an individuality as notable as that of William Byrd or Henry Purcell. It is impossible to live in the midst of the activities of English musical life without realizing that the wave is beginning to rise. Twenty-five or even fifty years may pass before the wave reaches its crest. But the upward movement is inevitable, and criticism should never be unmindful of this natural law.

CONTEMPORARY EUROPEAN MUSIC

NOT long ago Professor Weissmann, the well-known Berlin critic, published an article in which he discussed the separate influences of Schönberg and Stravinsky upon present-day musical creation, and in doing so revealed what to many of us has been a suspicion, and even a tentative conviction, that both these composers have already had their day. No sane person would be so rash as to assert that the development of music will proceed as smoothly and inevitably as if Schönberg and Stravinsky had never been born. In their different ways, they have even determined the course of that development to some extent. Yet, while admitting this, it is clearly evident that music as a whole and as a creative force has escaped their tyranny, and is no longer in direct contact either with their theories or their practice. Professor Weissmann mentioned certain important composers—Webern, Berg, Hindemith, Krenek, and Jarnach—who at some period of their lives have been strongly influenced by one or other of these principalities. But already it can be observed that the influence has been absorbed and made organic. There was a time when it acted like alcohol—raised the temperature, excited the imagination and the intellect, made the process of thought swiftly incoherent, and speech unintelligible. The excitement, such as it was, has passed, and theories have gone into the underworld of fixed habit. The younger European composers have a glorious opportunity. They are removed from the immediate reactions of war-psychology, and, with greater clarity than their predecessors, can speak the things they know. We have only to await the birth of a genius (as opposed to a merely superlative talent) to take advantage of the present time ' which now suits with it '.

To return to Schönberg and Stravinsky. What great and eloquent instruction we derive from their careers ! At different times, either could have claimed an almost universal homage. There never has been a time in the whole course of musical history when we needed definite leadership as urgently as now. It is most certain that if the truly beneficent Tyrant appeared, we should gladly follow and be subject, no less in the affairs of music than in the affairs of government. But, in music, we have been so often led away like sheep, that we have become wary and suspicious. The tyranny of Schönberg has brought no profit, no promise of consolidation. His ' transvaluation of all values ' is merely a denial of values, an elaboration of an empty, meaningless philosophy. His theorizing is as cheap and worthless as that of Boito's Iago. ' *E poi ? La morte è il nulla, è vecchia fola il ciel.*' As for Stravinsky, tyranny is too noble a word to apply to the pranks of this *enfant terrible*. Yet, in spite of their continued indifference to a power which was always ready to hand, both Schönberg and Stravinsky have been made Gamaliels by a few zealous disciples. And the zeal of these followers is so persuasive and compelling, that even now the musical public at large is always content and even eager to hear a new work from either of them. But the eagerness now is as nothing compared with that with which *Pierrot Lunaire* and *Sacre du Printemps* were awaited.

At Zürich not long ago, I was able to winnow an artificial enthusiasm in the expectation of hearing a work by Schönberg that I had not heard before. This was the *Quintet for Wind Instruments* (op. 26). But it had not progressed for more than ten minutes (a fifth of its course) before my enthusiasm fell like a dead leaf to the ground. I had prepared myself most carefully for the endurance of the ordeal. Earlier in the day, I attempted a synthesis of visual and aural perception by reading through a miniature score. There was promise in this. One could at least be aware of the diabolical ingenuity of it all. In the end I was enchanted by the intriguing designs and sequences impressed upon the pages. What an eye for music ! But when these patterns were projected upon the air, when the values were ' transvalued ', there fell a sudden great darkness upon my mind. The very essence of the process of musical thought was destroyed, and the rest was oblivion. Those meticulous figures and finely wrought details, which gave to the score the appearance of filigree-work, combined, when translated into sound, to annihilate all power of apprehension. It was not that I looked for beauty in this ingrowing music, for solace, for romantic warmth, and could find none ; for those who have at any time followed after Schönberg in his desert paths, have learnt to renounce these fleshly things, and, in denial, to pursue the lonely way without a backward thought. First he requires us to throw over the accepted melodic forms, then all the known systems of tonality, then all semblance of thematic material, and finally all notions of colour and instrumental idiosyncrasy. (To give example of this last phase, Schönberg's publisher told me that the composer was engaged upon the task of transcribing the whole of the *Wind Quintet* for strings.) And what have we gained by this great act of renunciation ? In vain we listen for the note of consistent authority. The *Wind Quintet*, so far from being authoritative, reveals a mind divided against itself. How can the house of Schönberg stand ?

And if Schönberg can be likened to an ill-founded house, Stravinsky calls up the image of a nomad's tent, which in stress of adverse weather can be conveniently folded up, carried away and pitched in more congenial environment. You can never be sure of finding it here or there. It has

no single path, no direction, no purpose, and,
belike, when you least expect to encounter it, it
will suddenly appear, flying a gay little French
flag overhead ; for a tent never takes deep root
and needs no foundation save the earth.   We did
not think to meet with it in London again ; but
that was the very best reason why it should
reappear.   M. Diaghilev was clever at picking out
psychological moments, and when he produced
Les Noces at His Majesty's Theatre, he did so with
malice aforethought.   The production had the
strangest effect upon the London public.   The
protests against the official verdicts of the critics
revealed that some curious inhibition had been
released ; plain, ordinary citizens wrote letters to
the Press and bared their minds quite shamelessly ;
wise men of astute judgement poured forth wild,
meaningless words with terrible vehemence.
Mr. H. G. Wells risked the reputation of a life-time
by issuing a little pamphlet, which I have read
many times, and still I am unenlightened as to
the nature of its impulse.   Another writer, well
known in certain circles, embarked upon a criticism
which caused me to blush for very shame.   Here
is an extract : ' Such an exhibition makes one
wonder whether Marinetti was not right after all ;
let us scrap all the old stuff, all the old masters,
and, having done away with the prejudices and
traditions born of them, give modern work a
chance of just appreciation.'   And again : ' To
any one coming to Stravinsky's ballet in a

receptive mood, the impression made upon him will be very different from that made upon the critics. The first thing that will strike him is the drastic realism of the whole affair. Here is something magnificently free from embellishment of every kind. . . . At times this relentless clarity of vision becomes almost unbearable. And the tensity of the poses and the cruel exultation of the music give us an aesthetic reaction, that is as strong and quite as exhausting as that brought about by an Ibsen drama or a symphony by Beethoven.'

I quote these sentences, not to confound the writer in his words, for he has confounded himself, but to give some indication of the reaction of quite a large number of people towards *Les Noces*. The reaction was primitive and passionate ; it led men to abjure their reason, and to give rein to hatred and violence. ' Was not this an evidence of power in Stravinsky ? ' you will ask. ' A man who can thus touch the instincts of his fellows is not lightly to be dismissed as of no account.' If so you think, you have overlooked an important point in the evidence. A man's power is to be judged not only by the extent (and after all the extent was comparatively small) but also by the nature of its influence. And I can discern no difference between the effect of *Les Noces* upon the London public as revealed in its written and spoken words, and the effect of a boxing-match in which the decision is given perforce on points. Both depend upon purely physical considerations.

Not all the official critics were offended by *Les Noces*. One spoke of ' masterly technique ' and ' powerful rhythm '. But how can these terms possibly be applied to a score which deliberately sets out (even more than in *Sacre du Printemps*) to emphasize one element of the product we call ' music ' to the exclusion of all the rest ? In *Les Noces* Stravinsky is obsessed with percussion. The pianos are used percussively, so are the voices, and so are the dancers ; and of the several kinds of drums it may be said that they are used repercussively. You may describe this reverberation as ' powerful rhythm ' if you like, but the fact remains that rhythm apart from its tonal, harmonic, and melodic context loses all significance, turns in upon itself and at length destroys itself. Can you conceive rhythm without song, and without the harmonic implications of all singing (whether vocal or instrumental) ? It is as impossible as the conception of song without rhythm, which has been the particular heresy of Italian opera for the last thirty years.

Moral : Put not your trust in intellectual ideals ; nor in composers who are for ever declaring their faith. By their works we shall know them. Both Schönberg and Stravinsky have at different times declared that they are seeking that elusive abstraction, ' pure music '. Stravinsky has disqualified himself, since it is obvious that he is not in a position to recognize his ideal, even if by any chance he pitched his tent upon its very ground. And Schönberg has so thwarted his creative impulse, that even if he discovered that which has been lost, he would have no power to breathe it into life and no means of clothing it with tangible form.

THE AUDACITY OF THE UNWISE

THERE are occasions when an idea presents itself with so much insistence, that there is no other way but to grant it immediate audience and discussion. Not long ago I met with a curious coincidence. During a period of reading I took up in turn a volume of Ruskin, a novel and a magazine. In all three I met with a different expression of the same thought. Ruskin put it in this way : ' Frankness is in itself no excuse for repetition, nor audacity for innovation, when the one is indolent and the other, unwise.' The novel was prefaced by this quotation from Josiah Royce : ' Revision does not mean mere destruction. We can often say to tradition, " That which thou sowest is not quickened except it die." But we can sometimes see in the world of opinion a sort of resurrection of the dead—a resurrection wherein what was indeed justly sown in dishonour, is raised in honour — glorified — and perhaps incorruptible. Let us bury the natural body of tradition. What we want is its glorified body and its immortal soul.' The magazine contained an article which made this quotation from Darius Milhaud : ' One of the purposes of the younger French composers is to preserve the older and more perfect musical

forms. . . . We are adding to the old harmonies.
We are expanding the old forms. But we are
not striving to do away with the established
order of things.'

Of late there has been an abundance of this
kind of justification. Words are easy, and
without casting the slightest suspicion upon
Milhaud's sincerity, we must beware of the kind
of statement he has made. Especially is it
necessary for composers to take heed lest they
deceive themselves with their ' after the event '
wisdom. What could be more simple than to
copy a Beethoven pianoforte sonata, with the
treble written out in the bass clef, and the bass
transferred to the treble, and call the result ' an
essay in adding to old harmonies, while still
preserving the established forms ' ? There are
people who entertain ideas as naïve as this,
amazing as it may seem. I could name a well-
known theatrical manager, a man with a very
shrewd sense of business, who imagined that, by
placing the pianoforte score of an old and established light opera before a mirror and copying the
reflection, he could produce a new and equally
popular composition !

It goes without saying that no contemporary
composer would be innocent or guilty enough to
catch a way so near as this. And yet, if the
truth were known, we should discover perhaps
that a few of them employ methods to which the
mirror device offers a rough parallel. There is

no insinuation here. This is not an accusation of forging and pilfering. The charge that I bring is far more serious, if only for the reason that composers are aware that it is more difficult to prove, and are therefore more easily persuaded to risk the condemnation.

In order to make my point in a musical manner, let me revert to a theme in a former essay :

' The creation of a work of music to-day differs altogether from the same process two hundred and fifty years ago. The composer then was not only creator but pioneer. The tendency of contemporary composers is to reverse these rôles, to concentrate upon the devising of a new form, or the expansion of an old one, and afterwards to seek for the idea that the form can conveniently accommodate. So it is that we encounter a number of systems and schools of composition, based on this scale or that chord, upon whole tones or quarter-tones ; and all these systems, as theories, are but confusion worse confounded, seeing that they are based upon the compromise of equal temperament. This fawning attitude of being only too willing to revere and employ traditional forms is only another aspect of the desire to destroy them utterly. It reveals a self-consciousness in composers which impedes their creative impulses. When, at the end of the sixteenth century, the development of the polyphonic style of music led to such complexity that it became almost incomprehensible, the reaction in favour of homophonic principles happened in the nature of things. There was no thought of attacking the old order ; nor was there any talk of pouring new wine into old bottles. The time for development had come, and those who were found wise and ready, took part in the movement without a backward thought.'

On every side we hear this tiresome note of self-justification. Every day the discovery is made that there is nothing new under the sun. The employment of parallel fourths and fifths by contemporary French and Russian composers is found to embody the same principle as the medieval *organum*. *Pierrot Lunaire* is compared with the French motets of the thirteenth century. Wagnerian chromaticism, we are told, was fore-shadowed and sometimes overshadowed by the adventurous madrigalists of early seventeenth-century Italy. False relations abound in ancient Armenian church music, and even the quarter-tone system was experimented with by Don Nicola Vicentino, a sixteenth-century Roman priest. ' You would condemn us for our spirit of adventure,' cry the eager young composers of our time. ' In reality we are returning to the very source of Music. We are breaking our servi-tude to the conventional ideas of tonality and striving to enter into a richer inheritance.' This is all very admirable, but unfortunately the calculation is upset by an important element—

one so important and constant indeed, that we often overlook its influence. However desirous we may be of achieving that spiritual state wherein Time is of no account, in the end we must always recognize its immense power. There are those who are inclined to belittle the music of the eighteenth and nineteenth centuries, because it was concerned with the exploration of a subsidiary system of tonality ; but, while it is possible to appraise the wide vision of these critics, it is necessary to realize the full significance of the fact that Music can never develop as if Mozart, Beethoven and Wagner had never existed. This may seem a platitude, but there are times when we are in sore need of its insistence.

The real weakness in the position of the present-day composer (regarding him as an impersonal sum of the outstanding composers of our time) is that of self-consciousness. It is a reflection of the age. Few composers can live and move and have their being to-day, without falling into the current ways of advertisement. Their creative work must of necessity lose spontaneity and freshness as a result. And, when we find as an exception a composer who is spiritually-minded enough to detach himself from the environment of his times, we perceive the same detachment and intense individuality in his work. Delius and his music afford an eloquent example. The self-consciousness which besets the majority of contemporary composers, leads them to surround themselves with a barrier of elaborate explanations and proclamations. Some even go so far as to explain their next new work before it is actually composed. The result is inevitable. Their work is no longer creation, but contrivance —an altered spelling. ' The new air does but make old decadences seem more stale.' In vain do they protest that they are seeking to preserve and enrich the established forms of composition. The protest is in itself a confession of failure, for that which is organically whole has no need of the attentions of self-appointed physicians ; and the more fluently they protest, the more evident is their lack of vocation.

PRINTED BY
JARROLD AND SONS LTD.
NORWICH